ARIZONA
LEGENDS

and LORE

tales of
Southwestern
pioneers

as told by
Dorothy Daniels Anderson
a master storyteller

Golden West Publishers

Cover design by Bruce R. Fischer / The Book Studio

Front cover original artwork by Cameron Daines

Library of Congress Cataloging-in-Publication Data

Anderson, Dorothy Daniels
    Arizona legends and lore / by Dorothy Daniels Anderson.
    Includes index.
    1. Arizona—History—Anecdotes. 2. Legends—Arizona.
    3. Folklore—Arizona.   I. Title.
F811.6.A54   1991   91-10594
979.1—dc20   CIP

ISBN 0-914846-55-8

Printed in the United States of America

Golden West Publishers   **(602) 265-4392**
4113 N. Longview Ave.
Phoenix, AZ 85014, USA

Golden West Publishers books are available at special discounts to schools, clubs, organizations and businesses for use as fund-raisers, premiums and special promotions. Send inquiry to Director of Marketing.

Acknowledgements

I wish to acknowledge my debt of gratitude to some special people who helped and supported me during the creation of this book. A special thanks to Wilhelmina Satina who questioned every trace of inconsistency in the stories and to Cheryl Byers who kept me within the bounds of good grammatical and language usage.

A deep bow of appreciation to all my fellow storytellers in the East Valley Tellers of Tales for their encouragement and positive criticism, with a particular thank you to Mary Wilson.

Thanks as well to all those lovers of history who toil in our museums and historical societies for their patient and good natured assistance, in particular: K. Trimble, Historian with the Phoenix History Project; Margaret Bret-Harte, Head Librarian, Arizona Historical Society, Tucson; Sue Abbey, Archivist, Sharlot Hall Museum; Jackie Engel, Arizona Historical Foundation, Hayden Library, Arizona State University; and Janet Michaelin, Librarian, Central Division, Arizona Historical Society, Phoenix.

Personal thanks to Harvey Leake and the Wetherill family for allowing me a special glimpse into family memorabilia.

A special round of applause to my sons: to Thor for his support and to Christian who gave me many hours of his time and challenged my thinking in every story.

Preface

There is a place that lies between daily routines and eternal truths. It is the place the storyteller comes from.

The task of the storyteller is to reach into the dreams, the knowledge, the thoughts of all who listen and find that thread of gold and spin it into a yarn, a tale that connects the then with the now, a tale that delights the spirit, a tale that lifts the soul.

Based on a quote from "Storyfest Ministry"
Robert Bela Wilhelm, Editor

Contents

Introduction

To settle in Arizona during the early days of its existence was to challenge life in a very elemental sense. Arizona was a place of extreme contrasts: long droughts, sudden rains, abundance and famine, dreadful heat and chilling cold. Survival was a struggle. Nothing was given, nothing could be assumed; nothing could be accomplished unless the individual found within him/herself the courage, the endurance, the stamina to succeed. Every day brought new hardships; every decision exposed new risks. Yet, like a magnet, Arizona attracted bold and free-thinking pioneers who came to try their luck against all odds.

Often in life, the catalyst of change is people. Pushed from their homes by a gnawing need to overcome the many deficiencies in their existence, pulled by a dream of the future, people changed Arizona through the desire to change their own lives.

The stories I have chosen for this book are about pioneers who came to this new frontier and greeted the harsh reality of the land as a challenge to overcome with enthusiasm. Their unique personalities captured for me the essence and soul of frontier life.

Some were well-educated doctors, lawyers, engineers, teachers. Others were barely literate. They came from every walk of life. Some succeeded, many more failed, but the stories of these pioneers echo the struggles of people throughout history and weave a fascinating tale of human adventure.

Sharlot Hall, Arizona's first woman historian, felt that "history is much more than a mere record of events, more than an accurate compilation of dates, names and places. True history must be the most vivid picture of past conditions that we can bring to the present and preserve for the future."[1]

Nothing expresses true history more vigorously than the tales of the people who lived it. To merely recount past events results in no more than producing a silhouette of human endeavor. It is the stories and inner thoughts of the pioneers that bring to history that vital aspect of

---

1. Sharlot Hall, Untitled speech, SHM Collection, Item 9, Document Box 8, Sharlot Hall Museum archives

emotion: the hopes, the fears, the triumphs, and the defeats.

Arizona Legends and Lore tells the stories of some of the most interesting and adventuresome pioneers in the early Arizona frontier. Each character is real and the events described are based on years of research through books, old journals, newspapers, magazines, talking with descendants of Arizona pioneers and going into archives of personal papers and memorabilia.

Only the most exciting, vivid and unique characters were chosen to be profiled in this book. Each story is a vignette in the life of one of these characters that provides the reader with an entertaining look at what made the Old West a land of legends.

Camels for Arizona

When a man joins the military, he might expect to encounter circumstances which demand great feats of heroism and bravery. Back in the rugged days of the early 1850s, Lieutenant Edward Fitzgerald Beale and Major Henry Wayne were two soldiers who certainly anticipated such encounters. Instead, what the military gave them was camels.

This is a story of a little-known footnote in history when the United States Army was faced with a perplexing problem. The military wanted to develop a supply route through the Southwest from Texas to California. But the land had scant water and little grass, and crossing the arid desert with mules and horses proved too difficult. What animal, what beast of burden could rapidly, with little water and food, carry large loads over this vast desert area?

In 1855, Jefferson Davis, the head of the War Department, was told by Congress to try a daring new idea. The plan was to import camels to the United States and use them for desert travel. Since camels were so successful in Egypt, Arabia, and Turkey, thought government strategists, surely they could also be used in the deserts of the Southwest. Thirty thousand dollars were appropriated for the project and in 1856 Major Henry Wayne was assigned the task of purchasing camels for the United States. Uncle Sam was in the camel business.

Now, not everyone thought that buying camels for the Army was such a wonderful idea. "Sounds like a hump-dinger of an idea to me," said one witty observer. "Those boys in Washington must have humps on the brain," quipped another. Most folks simply shook their heads in disbelief. Camels, those funny-looking humped things you saw in circuses! Could they keep up with horses? Could they carry as much as a mule? Would they need fancy foreign foods to eat? Would they work? The War Department was determined to find out.

Major Wayne's orders were simple. First, learn all you can about camels, then go to the Middle East and buy the best stock available.

The first place Major Wayne visited was the London Zoo in England. There he learned how camels adapted to living in captivity. Then he went to France and met with French soldiers who had used camels in North Africa. They told him how camels could be used for travel in harsh terrain. Next, he went off to Florence and Pisa, in Italy, where camels were bred by the royal Dukes of Tuscany. There he was shown that camels were tough beasts of burden who could easily adapt to extreme variations in climate.

When he finally reached the Middle East and started to buy camels, he discovered that most of his learning came from working with the animals themselves. Slick operators tried to sell him diseased, miserable old street-camels at outrageous prices. By necessity, Major Wayne had to learn a lot about camels very quickly and the more he learned, the more excited he became. Not only would camels solve the Army's problem but here was a wonderful new money-making opportunity for people in the United States.

He could see it all. Camels to carry thousands of pounds over arid desert lands. Camels to backpack cotton for Southern plantations. Camels to swiftly follow attacking Indians. Move over mules and horses; camels are going to revolutionize the American way of life!

The next challenge for Major Wayne was to get the camels to the United States. A Navy ship had been commissioned for the job, but getting thirty-three camels on board wasn't easy. The big dromedaries didn't take kindly to being pushed and shoved into strange places. The deck of the ship actually had to be cut away to provide enough head and hump room for them.

In spite of these difficulties and the Navy personnel's lack of experience, the camels arrived safely in Texas. In fact, a few births had even taken place during the voyage. Now the project was turned over to Lieutenant Edward Fitzgerald Beale. His assignment was to take the camels across the area now known as Texas, New Mexico and Arizona, and on to California through rough terrain and uncharted areas. If the camels could make it successfully, then a series of army posts would be established to relay mail and supplies across the Southwest.

At first things did not go well for Lieutenant Beale. His men did not know how to handle the exotic beasts and the camels were out of shape from their long confinement on board ship. But with the help of two handlers hired for the purpose, the Americans soon began to learn. The handlers were Greek

Embarking camels onto U.S. Naval ship bound for Arizona
(Courtesy Arizona Historical Society, Tucson, Arizona)

George and a man from Turkey named Hadji Ali. Hadji's name was much too complicated for the Americans to pronounce and he soon became known as "Hi Jolly," a name that was to stay with him for the next fifty years.

When Lieutenant Beale first accepted his assignment, he did so with a degree of good-natured humor. What else could he do about the situation in which he found himself? But as the journey progressed across the Southwest, his amusement soon changed to avid enthusiasm.

Camels were docile. Each could carry over a thousand pounds and travel forty miles a day without tiring. They ate anything available and seemed content with greasewood shrubs and cactus, plants no horse or mule would touch. They could also go for days without water and even ended up carrying water and food for the mules and horses when such items became scarce. They could travel faster than horses, swim swollen rivers, climb mountains and survive in conditions of two or three feet of snow. Everywhere Beale went people crowded around his dromedaries, fascinated. He became convinced that camels were the animal answer for the Southwest.

Predictably not everyone agreed. Initially, horses and mules stampeded at the sight of these strange animals. Handlers had to learn a whole different way to deal with them and often didn't care to learn. Nonetheless, by the end of the journey, the experiment appeared to be a success.

After such a promising beginning, have you begun to wonder why we don't see camels everywhere? Why are there no camel farms, camel shows and camel races in Arizona? Why are there no cowboys with their faithful companion, the camel? What happened?

Everything changed overnight. The long years of conflict between the Northern States and the South exploded into a Civil War. No longer could the military afford to keep isolated desert outposts for mail and supply service. Troops now needed for the war were withdrawn from the Southwest. Urgent military orders prevented Major Wayne and Lieutenant Beale from continuing to support these fascinating animals. In the confusion of war, camels were forgotten.

In time, a few were sold as pack animals, but the majority were simply allowed to escape into the desert. For many years they could be seen wandering in the foothills around the Gila and Colorado rivers. Eventually some were shot, some were captured, and some just disappeared.

Yet, the legacy of the camel experiment lingered on. About thirty years later, a camel was captured by a man from the Fort Yuma area. Here, he thought, was a way to make a little easy money. His scheme was to take the animal to Phoenix and sell it to the highest bidder. Surely someone would want to buy this exotic beast. But no one wanted to purchase his dromedary. Having invested considerable time and money into his venture, the man became desperate. What was he to do?

He owed money to a man in Phoenix and tried to give him the camel as payment for the loan. Knowing some information the other did not, the Phoenix man happily took the animal. A circus was scheduled to come into town in the next month. The new owner was certain that he could sell the camel to the circus and realize a handsome profit. Now all he had to do was take care of the animal until the circus arrived.

That task proved more complicated than anything he had imagined. He asked a friend if he could board his camel in the

Lt. Edward F. Beale, disguised as a Mexican for his perilous ride across Mexico bearing dispatches telling of the discovery of gold in California and a sample of the gold (Courtesy Arizona Historical Society, Tucson)

alfalfa field where the friend kept his mules. The man agreed and that evening the camel was put in the field. The next morning disaster met their eyes. Every mule, frightened by this uncouth alien, had tried to escape. Each was caught up in the barbed wire fence, while the camel was happily eating all the alfalfa in sight. The owner of the field promptly demanded that the camel be removed.

Next, the man decided to leave the camel in his own back yard. But that didn't work either. Every time the lady next door would attempt to drive by in her horse and buggy, the horse, upon seeing the camel, would rear up and try to jump into the buggy with the lady. She complained to the officials. The camel had to go.

The owner needed to come up with a new plan. Another friend of his owned a popular saloon next to which he kept a stable. Why not put his camel into the barn until the circus arrived? The animal could entertain the saloon's customers and hopefully stay out of mischief. But the barn door was not tall enough and no amount of pushing and shoving could persuade the camel to go inside. Eventually, the barn door had to be enlarged. None of this helped the disposition of his friend, or of the camel, who stayed sulking in the barn for a week refusing to eat or drink. Then one night, the camel proceeded to eat everything in the barn, including some bailing wire, kick open the door and escape down the street. After all these difficulties, the owner congratulated himself on being relieved of a major nuisance.

But the night had only begun and before it was over, that camel would be remembered in Phoenix for dozens of years.

The first incident occurred in the early morning hours. A rancher was bringing into Phoenix a wagon heavily loaded with hay. He had decided that he would test out a skittish new team of four mules. One moment he was quietly riding along the road, next to the canal, congratulating himself on his smooth handling of the team. The next moment he noticed some strange shambling object coming swiftly down the center of the road. That was the last thing he remembered until he awoke to find his mules hightailing it off in all directions and his wagon in the canal sinking fast.

A few minutes later, a little farther up the road, a butcher was driving a large herd of hogs to market. After months of carefully feeding and fattening his animals, he was dreaming, in the stillness of the early morning, of his impending profits. Suddenly, he caught a fleeting glimpse of something coming down the middle of the road like a stampeding tornado. Bare moments later, the butcher was left standing alone on the bank of the canal, viewing a hogless landscape. Distant grunts and terrified squeals came from all directions. For weeks afterward, the local newspapers ran articles of hog sightings from all over Phoenix.

Was it over? Not yet. Before the camel disappeared into the desert, he left a trail of upset buggies, frightened horses and irate citizens. As for the hapless owner, he quickly left town.

Are there any camels still left wandering our vast desert areas? Probably not. But the legend lives on.

Some say their ghosts remain. Occasionally, at twilight, one can see a huge red camel wandering out on the desert. On its back sits the bleached skeleton of a man, who many years before, dying of thirst, strapped himself onto the camel, hoping that even if he became unconscious, the camel would eventually lead him to water.

Others say that the ghost of a crazy old prospector can still be seen roaming the hills with his three faithful camels, loaded with a treasure of gold.

After the Civil War, the army never resumed its experimenting with camels. Railroads eventually solved the transportation problems across the Southwest. Time makes recollections vague, but until his dying day, the Turkish handler, Hi Jolly, swore that there were camels out there. Are some of their descendants still roaming our desert? I don't know, do you?

Camel expedition from photo of diorama in Arizona Historical Society
Exhibit Hall on "Camels in Arizona"
(Courtesy of Western Postal History Museum, Tucson)

BIBLIOGRAPHY

Eldon Bowman, "Beale's Historic Road: By Camel from the Zuni Villages to the Rio Colorado," *Arizona Highways*, July 1988, pages 9-18.

James E. Cook, "Riddle of Red Ghost Tormented Ranchers," *The Arizona Republic*, Sunday, April 17, 1988, E-2.

Sharlot Hall, "The Camels in Arizona," *Land of Sunshine*, March 1897, pages 122-123.

Sharlot Hall, "The Camels in the Southwest (A Forgotten Experiment)," *Out West*, XXVI, April 1907, pages 302-314.

Lewis Burt Lesley, "*Uncle Sam's Camels*," Cambridge, Harvard University Press, 1929.

Olive Oatman and a Massacre

Every nation at some point in time dreams of its future destiny.

In the mid-1800s America had such a dream. A dream that one day the country would double in size to span the territories between the Atlantic and Pacific oceans. With the Oregon Treaty of 1846 and the Mexican Cession of 1848, this vision became a reality.

Suddenly, from all over the United States, pioneers, with adventure in their hearts, began moving west. These settlers hoped to carve cattle ranches and farms from the wilderness, discover great treasures of mineral wealth, and build new lives. This is the story of one pioneer girl and her family as they traveled from Illinois to the newly opened areas of the Southwest.

Olive Ann Oatman lived with her parents, four brothers and two sisters on their small Illinois farm. Her father, Royce, was a good farmer and the family prospered until the failure of speculative banks and a depressed economy pushed them toward bankruptcy. The self-reliant Oatmans worked long and hard to overcome these difficult times, yet all their efforts were barely enough to make ends meet.

Then one desperate day, an overtired Royce Oatman did something that a man shouldn't do. He tried to lift a burden that was far too heavy for him. His back was so severely damaged that he had to spend several weeks in bed. In time, he seemed to get better, but the recurring cold of the Illinois winters triggered an inflammation in his back, which left Royce crippled up in pain and unable to work. During the summer, the pain would go away, but Royce's inability to work in cold weather further added to the family's hardships.

One day, while visiting a neighboring town, the Oatmans found a handbill announcing the formation of a wagon train going to the new territory of the Southwest. The handbill described vast tracts of land, perfect for farming and cattle ranching, available to anyone brave enough to make the journey and claim a homestead. In addition, it was prominently noted that the weather in these new territories was warm all year round. The family reasoned that if they could get Mr. Oatman to the Southwest, the warm climate would relieve him of his winter bouts of pain and a new homestead would give them the chance of future prosperity.

With the prospect of a new beginning, the Oatmans decided to join the wagon train. They sold their farm for $1,500 and bought a covered wagon, supplies and some cattle to take with them. In the summer of 1850, they departed for the Southwest.

At first, the trip was everything the Oatmans could have hoped for. The scenery was lovely; the weather was perfect, and every day was like a new adventure. As the families visited with each other, friendships formed and a feeling of confident expectation prevailed.

When the wagon train reached New Mexico, conditions changed. The land became a bleak, harsh, mountainous desert; it was harder to find water and grass for the overworked animals. Daily travel slowed to a crawl. In addition, several of the men were injured during raids by hostile Indians who badgered the wagon train, trying to steal horses and cattle.

With supplies dwindling, confidence in the expedition's success collapsed. Some of the families became discouraged and decided to turn back, but the Oatmans, determined to start a new life in the Southwest, pushed on.

As the pioneers crossed New Mexico and entered Arizona, more and more families deserted the expedition. When the settlers reached Tucson, their party had been reduced to eight families. With desperation showing in the eyes of many, and the realization that continuing the journey meant further hardships, only the Oatmans and two other families elected to go on. The now-shrunken expedition struggled northward along the Gila River.

When they reached a small Pima village near Maricopa Wells, the families stopped, exhausted, their food supplies dangerously low, their cattle lean and weak. The kind and gentle Pimas, who had been experiencing a drought, could share little food with the pioneers and their cattle. The families had to make a decision. Should they stay in the bleak conditions of the Pima village and nearly starve, killing their cattle to feed themselves, or should they push on across the desert to Fort Yuma, an area that promised the possibility of good grazing and farming land?

Their future lives at stake, the decision to stay or go on

weighed heavily on the minds of the settlers. With the news that Indians, hostile toward the land-grabbing white man, were attacking pioneers along their proposed route, the two families accompanying the Oatmans decided to stay in the Pima village.

Night after night, after the children had been put to bed, Mr. and Mrs. Oatman sat by their small campfire and talked about what to do. Every option was a calculated risk. Over and over they discussed the same issues: their lack of supplies, the rugged terrain to be crossed, the threat of Indian attacks. But was starving in the Pima village much better? There had been no Indian raids in over a month; was it now safe to cross the desert?

In the end it was not logic but hope which made the decision for the Oatmans. They chose to risk the trip to Fort Yuma with the same faith and optimism which had started them on their journey in the first place. The hope, the dream, the wish, that on the other side of struggle and hardship was a better life for themselves and their children.

Having made what modest preparations they could, the Oatmans offered assurances of a future reunion to their fellow travelers and departed for their destination. The trip was hard, but then they had known it would be; the terrain was rugged, but then it had been for several months. If there was anything which had changed for the Oatmans, as they struggled out across the desert, it was the expectation that this would be their final journey.

Still, as the miles of scorched, arid, desert land inched by, the family was pushed to the very limit of their endurance. At times the going was so rough that their wagon had to be fully unloaded in order to get it over or around some obstacle. Then began the arduous task of retrieving all their belongings, carrying them forward, and then putting them back into the wagon.

Despite the drudgery and feelings of total isolation, the Oatmans continued to persevere. Then on February 18, 1851, about ninety miles from Fort Yuma, the family was startled to see a group of Indians appear from behind a small hill. Uncertainty turned to alarm as the pale-faced Mr. Oatman watched the Indians approach.

At first these native Americans seemed friendly. They sat and gestured to him to join them in smoking a pipe. Speaking a few words of Spanish, they asked Mr. Oatman for food. Royce replied that his family of seven children and a pregnant wife did not even have enough to complete the trip to Fort Yuma. At this, the Indians grew angry, showing with gestures their need for food. Fearing for the safety of his family, Mr. Oatman gave the Indians half of his small supply. The Indians ate hungrily.

After they finished eating, they became angry again and demanded more food. Before Mr. Oatman could respond, one of the Indians grabbed two of his daughters, Olive who was thirteen years old and Mary Ann who was just seven, and dragged them over to some nearby shrubs. In front of the horrified girls' eyes, the other Indians took out clubs, hidden beneath their skin clothing, and began to attack the rest of the family.

Olive and Mary Ann, guarded by the Indian, were forced to witness the deaths of each member of their family. Some of the Indians rifled the wagon for food and a few light articles that appeared to take their fancy. Then the Indians turned toward the two girls. "This is the end," thought Olive. "Now it is our turn. Oh, God, please, let them get it over with quickly, I cannot bear to go on."

Rather than killing them, the Indians took the girls and fled the scene of the crime. The girls, numb with shock, were forced to run mile after mile into the desolate desert. Soon little Mary Ann became so fatigued she could run no further. She fell to the ground in complete exhaustion. One of the Indians began to beat her, but the fragile seven-year-old could not move. Traumatized from the brutal assault on her family, life had become meaningless; blow after blow fell unheeded on the fainting child. "This is it," thought Olive. "Now they will kill us. Please, God, let them get it over with."

Instead, the Indian threw Mary Ann over his shoulder and continued to run. Unsure of her sister's condition and now alone in her misery, Olive followed behind, her bare feet bleeding from the sharp rocks and thorns of the desert.

They continued to run for several days, stopping only for brief periods of uneasy rest. Exhausted beyond caring and having traveled over one hundred miles, the girls reached the Indians' village. Immediately the entire tribe surrounded them. Numb from the experiences of the last few days, Olive and the now revived Mary Ann were subjected to the tribe's anger. A fearful war dance began. The Indians spit on them, yelled at them, and made threatening motions toward them. "Now, they are finally going to kill us," thought Olive. "Finally, finally, it will be over."

Instead the Indians used the girls as slaves, making them forage for roots, cactus and seeds, carry water, and gather huge bundles of firewood. Whenever the girls did not understand the directions given them in the tribe's language, they were beaten. For food, they were forced to eat worms, grasshoppers, lizards, snakes, roots and only rarely were they given a bit of quail, rabbit or deer.

From the very beginning of their captivity, the girls made plans to escape. They would try to save food for the journey, but it was never enough. Soon Mary Ann, always the frailest of all the Oatmans, became too weak to make the attempt.

After a year of living a pathetic, hopeless existence, the girls' fate was unexpectedly changed. A strange group of Indians came to visit the tribe to trade for skins. Accompanying them was a tall beautiful Indian woman who seemed to be their leader. They were Mohaves. Before the girls realized what was happening, they were traded to the strangers for two horses, some beads, blankets and vegetables.

The Mohaves wrapped the girls' feet in skins for the long journey to their village. They traveled at a slow pace so that the girls could keep up and they fed them along the way. Such unexpected kindness during the ten-day trip made the difficult journey bearable.

When they arrived at their destination, the girls saw before them a beautiful valley near the Colorado River. They could see stalks of corn gently swaying in the breeze, the leaves of tall cottonwoods winked in the sun, and many of the hogans had thin streams of smoke rising invitingly from them.

Olive and Mary Ann discovered that the young woman who had led them over the desert was in fact the chief's daughter, and they were to live with the chief and his wife. Although they were still required to do much work for this Mohave family, they began to have hope for a better and kinder future. Indeed, the chief's squaw soon began to treat them like daughters. She assigned them their own plot of land to farm and she encouraged them to grow their own maize, melons and corn like other young Mohave women.

One day several of the members of the tribe, perhaps jealous of the attention given to the girls, accused Olive and Mary Ann of trying to escape. The Mohave medicine man tattooed each girl on the chin with marks similar to those worn by the women of the village. The Indians reasoned that this would permanently identify the girls as belonging to the tribe.

Even though they still felt fearful and alone at times, their lives were much better for well over a year. Then a severe drought occurred which caused much suffering and hardship among the Mohaves. The small stream that fed the farmland dried up. The corn stalks withered. The melons shriveled on the vines. At first the old people died and then the very little ones as food grew more and more scarce.

The chief's wife tried to help the girls when she could, by sharing what little food she had, but it was still not enough for the slight, fragile Mary Ann. Olive watched her sister slowly waste away. As little Mary Ann lay dying, she would sometimes sing the songs she had learned from her mother so very long ago. These sad little tunes touched the heart of the chief's wife and daughter, and when her sister died Olive asked to have her sister buried rather than burned in a pyre of dried wood, Mohave style. The request was granted. The Indians helped dig a tiny grave in the plot of land the girls had been given to cultivate. In an added gesture of generosity, Olive was given a blanket in which to wrap her sister's body.

Now sixteen years old, Olive was alone. As far as she knew, she was the only white girl for hundreds of miles. As the months passed by she wondered if she would ever see a white person again or ever know other people besides the Mohave Indians.

The drought ended after three years. The Colorado River flooded, filling the land and arroyos with rushing water. The melons and corn grew well and provided a fine harvest. A big feast to celebrate the return of better times was planned by the village.

Shortly after this time, a Yuma Indian messenger came to the tribe. He had a letter from the authorities at Fort Yuma. The commander of the fort wrote the chief saying that he had heard tales of a white girl being held captive by the tribe. The commander said that if there were any truth to the rumor he wanted the girl to be returned to her people.

This caused much consternation among the Indians and a council of the tribe's wise men was called to decide what to do. Should the white girl be returned for the gifts of blankets and horses? Would the white man come and attack them if they refused? Some said, "She is ours, we paid for her." Others said, "Let's kill her and pretend that we never had her." Olive's life hung in the balance as the tribe's council argued through the night. Finally it was decided to send Olive to Fort Yuma. But the Mohaves did not trust the Yuma messenger and sent the chief's daughter to accompany her on the long journey to the fort.

Many emotions tore at Olive Ann during the twenty days they walked, swam and floated along the Colorado River. It was a journey of over three-hundred miles. The tribe refused to allow her to take anything as a remembrance of the village. She found a few nuts and hid them in her skirt to try to keep something as a recollection of her life among these people, of the kindness of the chief's wife, and of the small plot of land where her dear sister lay. Those tiny, tiny nuts were to be treasured over many years.

As they neared the fort, the Yuma messenger sent a young Indian boy to announce that they were approaching. The boy explained to the authorities that the two young women were tired from the journey and could go no further. They had also requested clothes to dress themselves before entering the fort as they wore nothing but skirts of cottonwood bark.

After clothing and horses were sent with the young boy, people at the fort waited with apprehension for the girls to arrive. Many made murmurs of disappointment as they watched the two young women ride into the fort. Some said, "What charade is this?" Before them stood two Indian squaws, their dark faces showed clearly the Mohave tattoos. Then Olive Ann, who had kept her face downcast, raised her almost unbelieving eyes to look for the first time in five years at white people. The bright blue eyes peering out from the sunburnt face dispelled any doubt that she was anyone other than a young white woman. The occupants of the fort rushed excitedly to her side.

Much to Olive's delight and surprise, she learned that her older brother, Lorenzo, whom she thought had been killed along with the rest of her family, was alive and waiting for her. Lorenzo had suffered only a head injury at the time of the massacre and had been left for dead. He had managed to find help from some friendly Indians and had survived.

During the five years of Olive's captivity, Lorenzo Oatman had never given up the hope of seeing his sisters again. While visiting relatives in California, he repeatedly attempted to get help, to organize a searching party to look for his sisters. Everyone listened sympathetically to his requests, but no one believed that the Indians would have kept the girls alive.

Only Henry Grinnell, a carpenter at Fort Yuma, believed that the girls had a chance of survival. He made friends among the Indians and encouraged them to visit his cabin and share their news. Then one day, an Indian told him of a large celebration feast far north among the Mohaves and of seeing a white girl among them. Grinnell contacted Lorenzo and the commander of the fort.

In March of 1856, Olive was once again united with her brother and among her own people. The story of Olive's capture and rescue was the sensational news story of the day. Newspapers throughout the country wrote glowingly and romantically of her story.

Many believed that Olive survived only because she was strong from having lived an outdoors life as a farming girl. She was therefore able to withstand the hardships of living for so many years in primitive surroundings. Others felt that in those early years, the Indians had not yet suffered the extreme relentless destruction of their lives and lifestyle by the settlers. Had Olive been captured in later years, when the bitterness between these clashing societies had congealed into hatred, her fate would have been much different.

Olive and her brother left Fort Yuma and traveled to California, where they were able to attend school in the Santa Clara valley. A clergyman from the area, Reverend Stratton, wrote a book about her experiences. The book was an immediate success which gave Olive and her brother funds to continue their education. In March of 1858, Olive went east for further studies and to live with relatives in Rochester, New

York. There she met and fell in love with tall, handsome James Fairchild. They were married in November of 1865.

In time, they moved to Texas where James started the First Bank of Sherman, Texas and where Olive Oatman Fairchild lived out her days in a large, beautiful home built for her by her devoted husband. Her peaceful life was given to doing charitable works. She was particularly devoted to helping orphan children.

Olive Oatman after her release from captivity. Notice tattoo on chin.
(Courtesy Arizona Historical Society, Tucson)

Her sensitive understanding of the plight of these children was acknowledged by all who knew her. Having no children of their own, the Fairchilds even adopted one of these orphans who became their much beloved daughter.

Many who knew her during those years in Texas, before her death at the age of sixty-five, said she grew very shy. Rarely was she willing to meet strangers. Whenever Olive went into the town of Sherman, she would wear a large hat with a dark veil covering her face.

Olive Oatman Fairchild never returned to Arizona. Possibly she felt no need to. Every day, in spite of the countless washings, she could see when she looked into her mirror, those clear tattoo marks on her chin. Perhaps that looking-glass reflection reminded her all too vividly of her life among the Indians of Arizona.

BIBLIOGRAPHY

Arizona Development Board, *Amazing Arizona: Historical Markers in Arizona*, Vol. 1, 1521 West Jefferson Street, Phoenix, 1960.

Dr. Al Daniels, descendant of the Oatman family, interview, 1987.

J. B. Fairchild, Letter to Sharlot Hall, The Commercial National Bank, Sherman, Texas, December 21, 1905.

Sharlot Hall, "Olive A. Oatman—Her Captivity With the Apache Indians, and Her Later Life," *Out West*, July to December, 1908, pages 216-227.

Major Samuel P. Heintzelman, Original journal from January 1, 1851-December 1853, "Concerning the establishment of an army post at the junction of the Colorado and Gila rivers." Yuma County Historical Society.

Olive Oatman, Original lecture notes used in her speeches, Arizona Historical Society, Yuma.

Reverend Edward J Pettid, S.J., "The Oatman Story," *Arizona Highways*, November 1968, pages 4-9.

Reverend Royal Byron Stratton, *The Captivity of the Oatman Girls,* San Francisco: Whitton, Towne and Company, 1857.

Olive Oatman Fairchild's residence in Sherman, Texas
(Courtesy of Sharlot Hall Museum Archives, Prescott)

No Tame House-Cat Woman

As the first white child to be born in Lincoln County in the territory of Kansas in October 1870, Sharlot Hall never saw another child during the early years of her life. Her only playmates were some buffalo calves her father had captured on one of his hunting trips. In spite of their enormous size, they became quite tame. She helped to feed them and loved to push her face into their long, rough coats of fur. They, in turn, lumbered behind this little girl of the prairie, following her wherever she went.

Sharlot's mother, a former school teacher, had married James Hall when she was twenty-two years old, after her family had come to Kansas to homestead. Sharlot was their firstborn. For a long while, the only woman Sharlot knew was her mother. As a small child, Sharlot followed her mother everywhere: to feed the chickens, weed the garden, wash the clothes and to bake bread in a Dutch oven in their cabin's large fireplace.

As isolated as they were, Adeline Hall did not ignore her daughter's education. She wanted Sharlot to know that there was a much larger world out there beyond the ranch. When the chores were done she began to teach three-year-old Sharlot all she knew. In those days there was very little reading material available out in a secluded homestead. They had two books which came from Adeline's father, Grandfather Boblett. So Sharlot's first reading primers were the daunting texts of the *Library of Mesmerism* and the *Phrenological Journal.*

Sharlot didn't always understand what she read, but she loved sounding out the words. What mattered was to say them, rolling them trippingly off her tongue. There were other books, her mother said, that told stories about people's lives.

James Hall was a product of the frontier, with only minimal schooling. He did not trust educated people, his wife being the only exception. Occasionally Sharlot's father would read stories to her from a *Farm and Ranch* magazine. She soon noticed that all the stories seemed the same. The hero was always the noble farmer and the villain was always the doctor, the lawyer or the clerk, the educated person. She wondered if all stories had the same patterns, told over and over again.

When other pioneers moved into the area, Sharlot soon discovered that all the frontier settlers seemed to distrust educated people. On those rare occasions when groups would gather for a visit, Sharlot would try to explain about her love for reading, her sense of wonder over words, but the response was always the same. "What does a farm girl, a ranch girl need with reading? No call for it, just trying to have high-faluting ways."

Sharlot learned to accept the work of the farmer's life, doing it well so as to forestall any punishment, like the taking away of her precious books. Her hands took on a swift skill. She accepted the fact that what was needed was for her to hang up the saddles, wire the gates shut against roving calves, cut wood for the stove and cook meals. Books and poetry were for high-toned people, not for the rancher, not for a farmer's daughter. She was afraid to ask where such people lived. She knew it must be somewhere very, very different from the open prairie of Kansas.

Then, one evening, some neighbors came over to the cabin for a social visit. In the course of the evening, they began to talk about this old, odd man, Mr. Cushion, funny kind of name, who lived in the area. The visitors said that he shut himself up in his cabin for days with all those books of his, then he'd go wandering around the hills by himself all the time.

Everyone began to laugh and make fun of Mr. Cushion, except Sharlot. She became determined to meet Mr. Cushion and to somehow get him to allow her to read his books. Was he high-toned? Why then did he live in a cabin in Kansas?

For days she would watch his cabin after she had completed her chores. When he went for walks, she would follow him, ever careful not to be seen. She had to figure out a way to get him to let her read his books. But it did not appear to be an easy thing to do. Mr. Cushion didn't seem interested in nature; he never laughed or sang or whistled. Did he hate everybody? Is that why he shunned all the neighbors?

Her determination soon yielded to desperation. What could she do? What could she say? Finally one day, she could bear it no longer. She jumped out some twenty feet in front of him on the trail.

"My name is Sharlot Mabridth Hall," she shouted. "I read books. I have read the *Library of Mesmerism* four times and the

Phrenological Journal six times!" Surprised, Mr. Cushion stopped and looked at the determined little eight-year-old girl before him, her anxious face staring into his. "Folks around here say you're crazy to have all those books, but I don't think so," she said. "I think you must be the richest man in the territory of Kansas to own all those words."

Then her precious words failed her and she stood trembling, unable to move, waiting for this man to decide her fate.

Finally, after what seemed like an eternity of waiting, he said, "So you like to read, Sharlot Mabridth Hall; then you'd best come to my cabin and show me just how well you can read."

Sharlot's heart soared. From that point on, Mr. Cushion, that wonderful odd old man, lent her books. She read quaint old histories and books on philosophy. She read Kant and Swedenborg. It didn't matter to her that she did not always understand it all; she loved the words.

Then James Hall decided that Kansas was getting far too crowded for him. He liked space without the encroachment of people. Sharlot's uncle, her mother's brother, wrote from the territory of Arizona describing the open empty land that was there for the taking. They were to move to Arizona.

As a going-away present, Mr. Cushion gave Sharlot two books. These were the first books she ever owned and she treasured them. One was a book of poems by Bret Harte. Whenever she had completed her chores, she would go out in the fields and hills by herself and read those poems out loud to the birds, the rabbits, the farm animals. To write poetry would be the most wonderful thing that a person could ever do. The other book that the old scholar gave her was completely unsuitable for a young girl, but she treasured it anyway. It was Daniel Defoe's *The History of the Devil.*

For Sharlot, the trip to Arizona was exciting. She reveled in the constantly changing scenery, the sense of freedom. Because the family would be traveling on public thoroughfares, Sharlot's father insisted that she ride sidesaddle, rather than the usual astride and bareback that was permitted in the confines of the farm.

One day, instead of paying attention to her horse, Sharlot spent her time looking out for the possibility of finding a small left-over nugget of gold on the way. She had heard stories of gold being discovered in Arizona. All she wanted was one small nugget, just enough to buy herself some books. Intent on her search, she allowed her horse to wander with too loose a rein. The horse spooked at something and threw her off. She landed flat on her back, injuring her spine so severely that she was plagued with back problems for the rest of her life. She did not tell anyone of her fall. Fearful of getting punished, she got back on the horse and rode with the pain for days.

The Hall family camped out on the ranch of Uncle John Boblett, while Sharlot's father looked around for suitable land on which the family could settle. While at Uncle John's place, the family went to visit the town of Prescott, located some ten miles away. At that time, Prescott was the largest town in the territory after Tucson.

Prescott was the biggest town Sharlot had ever seen. It had a theater, a concert hall, a new city hall, two banks, two schools, three newspapers, four stables, five churches and eighteen saloons. The veneer of culture was in strong competition with the needs of the miners and cowboys who lived within reach of the town. Prescott even had a railroad going through it and it also had regular stagecoach service. The only problem with the stage was that it was prone to getting robbed. Bandits would swoop down on the unsuspecting passengers, strip them of their valuables and then vanish into the surrounding mountain wilderness.

Occasionally, the sheriff would catch one of these desperadoes. Then there was always a hanging. Hangings inevitably took place on Saturday. The *Weekly Arizona Miner*, one of the local newspapers, consistently featured an article in Monday's paper full of all the details of the hanging. Over the years, Sharlot, who had a knack of noticing all sorts of things, began to realize that the articles always ended in the same way, with many compliments to the sheriff for having made the occasion such a pleasant one for everybody. The harsh realities of frontier life were often tempered by her humorous view of the world as she saw it.

James Hall finally located a piece of land for a ranch some fifteen miles from Prescott, in an area called Lonesome Valley. It suited her father admirably for it was indeed an isolated place. Ranching was wonderful that first summer. There was plenty of rain so the grass was abundant and the streams held rushing water. Cattle prices were high. Sharlot's father made money that year and invested the money in even more cattle.

About that time, when Sharlot was twelve years old and her brother was nine, they were allowed to attend school for the first time. The little school was about four miles from the ranch. The brother and sister rode their horses there every day. They wrote their lessons on slates that were trimmed in red felt. Sharlot was fascinated by everything about school. By this time she had decided that she was seriously going to try to be a poet and a writer. But where to find the time? After school, every spare minute was taken up with chores on the ranch. Instead of doing her geography lesson, Sharlot would often write verses in her little notebook. Of course she tried to make her poems about geography and history. She wrote poems about Florida and Christopher Columbus. She could not help herself, she just had to write.

One day, after Sharlot had been at school only a term, Miss Johnson, her teacher, summoned her father for a parent conference. Sharlot sat in the corner of the schoolroom trembling, reviewing in her mind all the sins and omissions of her days at the school.

"Mr. Hall," her teacher began, "Sharlot has been with me for a term now and she has learned everything that I know to teach her. She is ready to go to the big school in Prescott. Judge Howard's wife is looking for a girl to help around the house and is willing to give Sharlot her room and board and allow her to attend school. Sharlot can go home on weekends to help on the ranch."

Sharlot could not believe what she had heard. But she did not dare to hope that such a thing would happen, for she knew her father. He did not like educated people and their high-toned ways. He would never let her go. But she had not reckoned with pretty Miss Johnson's persuasive ability. After a brief thoughtful silence, James Hall agreed to allow Sharlot to go to school in Prescott.

Living at the Howards, and attending school, Sharlot experienced some of the happiest moments of her life. She stayed at school in Prescott for eight months. Never before had she had friends, children her own age, to talk to or sometimes simply to listen to. Then her mother became very ill and Sharlot had to return to the ranch to take on her chores. That was all the formal education that Sharlot was ever to have.

If her mother's illness was not problem enough, even greater tragedy struck. A drought descended on the area that was to last for four years. The streams dried up. The grass dried up and blew away. The cattle were pitiful. Many of them died. Each day Sharlot had to learn to do hard things to keep the family from starving. Years later, Sharlot wrote a poem about those days of the drought. Many people from all over the country wrote her telling her how much that poem explained how they felt.

And then it began to rain. It rained for over a month. Much of the ranch was flooded. By this time Sharlot's father decided that ranching was no way to make a living. He decided to join his brothers-in-law and do some hydraulic mining of gold flecks found in the bluffs of creeks and streams. They staked out some mining claims in the Lynx Creek area. For the next few years Sharlot, her father and uncles mined the creek. Sharlot's mother was too ill to join them.

It was hard, hard work in cold weather. Sharlot was chief cook and keeper of the gold bullion. Not a door in their cabin would lock, so she always slept with a big revolver under her pillow and tried to keep an eye open at all times looking out for bandits. From her youthful perspective, it was an exciting life always having to be on the lookout for a possible raid, especially after a clean-up when there was plenty of gold stored.

Sharlot's father eventually amassed enough money to build a good-size house on the ranch in Lonesome Valley. It was the largest house around and well-built. Her family decided not to go back to ranching but instead planned to plant fruit trees— apples, pears, peaches. Fresh fruit was a scarce commodity in those days and would fetch a good price among the miners and townspeople.

Lots of the old-timers laughed at the family when they heard that they were planting fruit trees. No one believed that such a type of tree could grow in that altitude and, if that were not problem enough, there was not sufficient water available to nurture them. The old-timers were right about the water. The trees on their newly-named Orchard Ranch grew small, but they eventually did bear their precious fruit.

Sharlot continued to live on the ranch to help out her constantly ill mother. It was a hard life for a young girl blossoming into womanhood. There were rarely any visitors. While other young girls of her age in towns like Prescott were often caught up in the social whirl of church activities, dances and visiting, Sharlot's life was that of a busy ranch woman. It was up to her to keep up with the orchard, garden, chickens and the housework.

Sometimes she keenly felt the total isolation of ranch life. These were the bad times when her loneliness brought on such feelings of despair. It was then that she started to write letters to the authors she was reading, particularly to those authors who wrote about their own experiences dealing with loneliness. She treasured the few letters that authors would write back to her.

One of her most precious was from Rudyard Kipling. He wrote something that Sharlot committed to memory to help during the times when she needed consoling the most.

I used to know a little about loneliness in the heat and dust of India and I know what a comfort it is to be taken out of real things for awhile by reading a book.[1]

About that time Sharlot discovered that people would actually pay her to write. She sold her first article to a children's magazine. She received a payment of four dollars. That was a lot of money in those days when people often worked for ten cents an hour. The story was a description of a Moqui (Hopi) folk tale. Sharlot began to realize that writing might be a way for her to earn money to help out with the ranch. Apparently people in the eastern sections of the country were fascinated with everything about western ranch life and the Indians. There was a market for articles about these things. She took to visiting local Indian ruins so that she could write knowledgeably about them. She enjoyed the sense of freedom that even a small excursion offered her.

Sharlot also began to enter every writing contest that she could find hoping that if she could win, not only would she receive a gift or money, but it would enhance her status in submitting her work for financial remuneration. She won a dozen prizes in a three-year time. She won one hundred dollars

Sharlot Hall as a young woman seated at the Blickensderfer typewriter
(Courtesy of Sharlot Hall Museum, Prescott)

from the Aeromotor Company in Chicago. The family bought more fruit trees with that money. She also won a Blickensderfer typewriter. Now she began to feel that she had a profession as a writer. Her life on the ranch now had fewer moments of lonely despair. Perhaps writing would be her pathway to freedom.

She wrote about everything she saw and knew concerning what life was like in the West. She wrote about living on a ranch. She began to write poems in earnest for publication.

Then Sharlot heard about a new magazine from Los Angeles called *Land of Sunshine* edited by Charles Lummis. She started submitting poems and articles to Mr. Lummis. For the first time, Sharlot had an editor who took a personal interest in her as a writer. He encouraged her to write for his magazine. He carefully critiqued her work, demanding rewrites for material that was not yet acceptable. Her work for the magazine brought her national recognition as a fresh vital voice from the West. Her relationship with Lummis as her editor was to last for years.

Isolated as she was on her secluded ranch in the Territory of Arizona, continuing still to do all the gardening and bossing of ranch hands, Sharlot was now a published writer. Suddenly it was her turn to receive letters from people who had read her work. On one occasion, a man wrote to her to inquire how a mere woman could have acquired such a marvelous vocabulary as her writing revealed. Always one to find humor where she could, Sharlot wrote back that one winter on the ranch the only new book in the house that she had to read was the dictionary.

Charles Lummis invited Sharlot to visit him in Los Angeles, where she met many of his literary friends and associates. It was an exhilarating time for a young ranch woman to travel to the coast and to meet so many prominent writers and artists. Her unblinking, clear-eyed ranch woman's vision let nothing slip by her. These were indeed the high-toned people of her childhood wonderings. The quiet Sharlot found herself welcomed and accepted. People began to refer to her as the Western poet who knew how to write about her colorful life in Arizona.

Besides her writing and poetry aspirations, Sharlot began to set other goals for herself. She wanted to record the lives of the early Arizona pioneers before the information about them was lost. She would write their stories. She would preserve their tales. She would try in every way she knew to see that these pioneers would be remembered.

Mr. Lummis wanted Sharlot to move to California. He wanted her to become a permanent member of the staff of his magazine, now called *Out West*, newly named after the title of a poem she had written. Here was an offer of a chance at freedom, to finally get away from the incredibly hard labor of the ranch, away from the constant, persistent responsibility. How she yearned for that freedom. All those isolated years on the ranch, when she dreamt of that almost impossible dream. Here was the opportunity to be free, to travel, to meet people, to do all the wonderful things that dreams are made of.

Several times Sharlot went out and worked on the staff of the magazine. She even began to look over various parcels of property with an eye to purchasing. But her mother had no love for California, her father wanted only the isolation of Lonesome Valley. Somehow each opportunity to remain in California always ended with a return to the ranch. She began to realize that she was after all an outdoors woman. She could not bear to stay away for too long before she had to see those pinyon pines, the stark but beautiful mountains and desert, the freeing, untamed wilderness. Possibly she was more of a dutiful daughter than she had been willing to admit to herself. Her parents were frail. They needed her help. She had to stay.

Sharlot did continue to visit Charles Lummis and his family in Los Angeles whenever she could. Those visits were for her a window to a wider intellectual world more varied in color than the reading of her precious books could give her. During one of those visits, she met with a group of people who were trying to establish an archaeological museum in Los Angeles in order to collect and preserve artifacts from the early days of California.

With a flash of insight, Sharlot realized that their objective gave added direction to her life's ambition. Not only would she record the stories of these pioneers who lived in Arizona, she would collect the artifacts used by these early peoples. These artifacts, from the homespun pioneer possessions to rare and ancient Indian objects, would add a dimension to the stories. To conserve these things would give future generations a compelling sense of the people who walked, lived and loved on this land so long ago. Sharlot decided then that she must work toward the creation of a museum for Arizona artifacts.

Once, returning from a California visit, her mind busy with new plans for achieving her goals, she found Arizona's very existence threatened. A bill had just been introduced into Congress, called the Hamilton Bill, which proposed that the territory of Arizona and the territory of New Mexico be once again joined and come into the United States as one state. The citizens of both territories, recognizing an imminent identity crisis, were outraged. Petitions and strong arguments fell on deaf congressional ears. The motives of Washington were simple political expediency. To sustain a balance of power toward eastern states the Senate wished to limit the number of new western states. The desires of a small population in a sparsely settled area was of little interest to the powerful forces that ruled Congress.

Sharlot felt she had to do something to help keep the Hamilton Bill from passing. She decided to interview as many people as she could to garner opinions about the feelings of Arizonans for the Hamilton Bill. She would then write an article expressing the results of her interviews. She knew that Charles Lummis would publish such as article in the *Out West* magazine. In fact, he wished to devote an entire issue to this crisis. This would give the nation an opportunity to listen first-hand to the voices of the people living Arizona.

With a surge of frenetic energy, Sharlot spoke out against the Hamilton Bill at the annual convention of Arizona women's clubs. She traveled around the territory amassing interviews and information. She worked so hard, missing meals, losing sleep, traveling in bitterly cold weather, that she became quite ill. Alarmed that she was coming down with that killer disease, pneumonia, she felt she had no option but to return to the ranch and try to get well.

While on the train back to Prescott, she happened to notice the headlines of a newspaper being read by a fellow passenger. "Joint Statehood Ordered, President Teddy Roosevelt Directs Congress To Annex Arizona." She was stunned. How could the President make such a recommendation in the face of so much opposition from citizens in both territories? Her thoughts and emotions were wild and jumbled on that cold and tedious train ride.

She didn't arrive back at the ranch until ten o'clock that night. Adeline Hall took one look at her daughter and became frightened by how ill she looked. "Sharlot, my dear, you must go to bed at once."

But Sharlot was a-tremble with emotions, arguing words, indignant words, fighting words, struggling to come out.

"Mother," she said, "make a fire in the sitting room for me. Please make me some tea and go to bed and leave me alone. Please, Mother, I've got a poem to write before I turn in. The opening lines have been singing in my head for hours on the train home. I must write. I simply must write."

Sharlot grabbed some paper. She had to write of her feelings about Arizona losing its hard-won identity. She had to somehow express the emotions of all the people she had interviewed who felt as passionately as she did.

> *Arizona is no beggar in that mighty hall where her bay-*
> *crowned sisters wait,*
> *No empty-handed pleader for the right to be a free-born state.*
> *No child, with a child's insistence, demanding a gilded toy*
> *No! But a fair-browed, queenly woman with land too strong*
> *to destroy.*[2]

She wrote like a fury all through the night. Her poem was eight stanzas long. By morning it was completed. Instead of feeling drained and exhausted as well as weak from her illness, she discovered that she felt fine. Further than that, her cold was gone. She wondered with an inward chuckle if all those germs simply could not survive in a body so charged with anger and indignation.

As soon as Sharlot had taken a rest, she typed a good copy of her poem on the Blickensderfer, and went back to Phoenix. She showed the poem to Dwight Heard, publisher and owner of the *Arizona Republican* newspaper.

A delegation of twelve prominent men had been chosen to go to Washington and argue for Arizona. Mr. Heard, one of the delegates, read Sharlot's poem and published it in the editorial section of his newspaper. Many people wrote to the paper praising the poem for expressing their anger at what was about to happen to the territory.

"Sharlot," Heard inquired, "may I make extra copies and take your poem with me to Washington?"

"Of course, do anything that could help," she replied.

Dwight Heard decided to give a copy of the poem to every member of Congress to read and, he hoped, begin to understand the feelings of the people living in the territory. Sharlot's poem was even read into the Congressional Record.

But things looked hopeless. The Hamilton Bill was rammed through the House of Representatives, 192 to 165 votes. Surely the Senate would follow suit. It appeared as if it were all over. The territory of Arizona was to become a part of the state of New Mexico. Sharlot wondered if anyone in future years would even remember that there had once been a place called Arizona. The *Out West* magazine finally came out with an entire issue devoted to the Hamilton Bill and its effect on Arizona. Sharlot had written a sixty-four page article expressing the potential of the territory.

Whatever influences finally convinced the senators will never be fully known. But the part of the Hamilton Bill pertaining to joint statehood for Arizona and New Mexico was stricken from the Senate version. Arizona and New Mexico were allowed to remain separate territories until such time as it was deemed appropriate to grant each the right to enter as an individual state. Sharlot Mabridth Hall had made a significant contribution to the continued existence of Arizona as an independent entity.

Back at the ranch once again, Sharlot felt she could now return to her twin ambitions: to create a museum of Southwest artifacts and to collect for history the stories of those early pioneers.

One such pioneer was Charles Genung, an old-time rancher. Sharlot had met Mr. Genung and began, through an exchange of letters, to learn about his life when he first arrived in Arizona. She was particularly interested in his descriptions of his first year, when he and two companions had located a small gold mine and were busy taking out ore.

Charles Genung invited Sharlot on a sentimental journey by traveling wagon to trace the route he had originally taken when he entered Arizona from California. Sharlot thought such a trip would be an excellent opportunity to meet some of his old mining and sheepherding buddies and listen to their stories and experiences about Arizona during those early days. And so she went with this grandfatherly man who loved Arizona enough to undertake a rugged journey for remembrance sake. His wife and their seven grown children and their families chose to stay home.

When Sharlot wasn't traveling around the territory gathering information for articles, she was often speaking at women's clubs, sharing with women her pioneer stories, reading to them her poems and always asking them to take on the task of helping to finance a museum for the collection of Arizona artifacts.

On January 7, 1907, Prescott's Monday Club hosted a gala Hassayampa Evening at the Opera House. Sharlot told the audience about Arizona's earliest history when the first territorial governor, John Goodwin, established the capital at Prescott. "There still stands one rare monument of those early days," she said. "It is the old Governor's house." That night she proposed that funds be found or set aside to preserve that priceless relic for future generations who would want to know what it was like in those olden days.

Many of the women in those clubs gave Sharlot invaluable help. But there were the other women who frowned on her free ways. Here was a woman without a husband, no older woman companion or relative to accompany her, who traveled around the territory with various men, interviewing men, camping out in rough, wild territory with no one around but men. A newspaper in Agua Fria once wrote an article of her visit to the community's society for women by stating that Miss Harlot Shawl had given a speech that week. The paper said that it was just a typographical error.

Little did these women understand. For them the only possible reason Sharlot would leave the proper sphere of a woman, the home, would be to fling herself at every male that she met in the territory.

Sharlot was glad that God had let her be an outdoor woman. She gave thanks for her eyes that could see the beautiful, the glorious things of this land. She knew deep in her heart that she could never be a tame house-cat woman spending those wonderful sunny days that Arizona is so blessed with giving card parties and planning dresses. Not that she didn't love pretty clothes, good dinners and friends. She did. How she would have loved a home where only true and worthwhile things had a place. But in the meantime she had a vision, a dream that needed doing and she would do it as best she could.

Perhaps those women would have been satisfied had Sharlot been married. But she had lost the great love of her life when she was in her twenties. His name was Samuel Porter Putnam. Samuel had come to Prescott when twenty-five-year-old Sharlot was a young aspiring writer. Son of a congregational minister, he also became a minister. Later in his life, he became an advocate of the principles of freethought. Considerably older than Sharlot, Samuel Putnam had come to Prescott to give a series of lectures on this popular philosophy of the time.

Freethought espoused the concept that people should be free in every aspect of their lives and in particular in the relationships between men and women. In Prescott at that time, as in most frontier environments, women were still considered virtual slaves of their fathers, brothers and husbands. Samuel Putnam spoke of bringing the Republican spirit into the home by creating an equality between man and woman, between husband and wife. To freedom-loving Sharlot, it was like glorious music to her ears to hear a man talk of equal rights for men and women in all walks of life. How she cherished his words when he said that "if there is to be real love between a man and a woman there must be liberty. The moment authority of one over the other occurs, liberty disappears and is lost forever."

Samuel and Sharlot struck up a close friendship while he remained in Prescott. They continued their friendship by corresponding to each other for several years. Sharlot felt that their letters revealed an ever-deepening relationship that would one day blossom into a blessed union. But then Samuel died unexpectedly under dreadful circumstances. She was devastated by this loss and mourned him for years. To help overcome her grief, Sharlot worked even harder at writing than ever before, consoling herself with the thought that perhaps their companionship had been too perfect, their hopes, plans and happiness too great to be realized on this earthly plane.

Because of Sharlot's ever-increasing publicity as a writer and her help in blocking the Hamilton Bill, she was eventually offered an opportunity to receive a clerkship in the Arizona Territorial Legislature. Since Sharlot was interested in history, Charles Lummis suggested that she take the job because it would give her a chance to catch history alive while it was happening. She was paid three hundred dollars for the two-and-a-half months she worked during the legislative session. That was good money in those days. That was wonderful money for a ranch woman from Lonesome Valley.

With the support of the various women's clubs and many friends from the territorial government, she was appointed by

Governor Richard E. Sloan to become the territory's state historian. She was the first woman to hold a public office of this stature.

Sharlot took her position of territorial historian with great seriousness. She was determined to use this opportunity to travel the length and breadth of the territory gathering information to compile into a systematic set of files as sources of reference for people who wished to have explicit knowledge of the area during the early pioneer times. She soon became extremely busy, as no one had attempted to do anything of this dimension before.

She personally interviewed many of the survivors from those first days when the area was opened up for settlement. She felt that these interviews, coupled with the facts and figures about the area, would give future generations a multi-layered sense of a by-gone time. She spent nearly two months traveling in southern and eastern Arizona.

During her tenure in public office, Sharlot undertook one of the longest and most exciting expeditions of her life. She took a wagon trip north of the Grand Canyon into an unknown area isolated from the rest of the territory by the then-impassable barrier of the Colorado River. This land was known as the Arizona Strip. The few Mormons who had settled there felt closer ties to Utah than to Arizona and they had petitioned Congress to allow the section to be annexed to Utah. Sharlot hired a guide to take her there in order to see if there was anything of value in the area for Arizona, before such an action should be taken.

Sharlot was an outdoor woman used to rugged conditions, but this was the hardest trip she had ever undertaken. In places there were no roads and trails were often a mere figment of the imagination. They had to carry not only their own supplies on just one wagon, but most of the feed for the horses. Much of the time she walked in front of the horses to guide them, as well as to lighten the load of the wagon through the sand.

She was bitten by swarms of mosquitoes. She slept on earth that was as hard as a bed of iron. When, with her special sense of amusement, she recalled those nights, Sharlot always said she had no need of a professor of anatomy to tell her how many bones she had. The bones themselves gave her a complete listing through the long and sleepless nights. Yet in spite of the hardships, she fell in love with that silent, mystical, vividly colored, unearthly land.

On the trip, she steeped herself in the history of the place and its stories. She visited the graves of the men killed in the Indian wars. She learned about James White's voyage through the Grand Canyon in 1867. She pored through records in the Kingman courthouse. She wrote a book about her trip, describing the country and indicating the vast resources that were there waiting for Arizona to develop.

When her tenure was over, she had hoped to be reappointed to the position so that she could continue the work she felt so strongly about. But political considerations resulted in the job being given to someone else. There was nothing else to do but to return once again to the isolation and responsibility of the ranch. Sharlot did manage to get published a book of poems called *Cactus and Pine*.

Then, on August 24, 1912, when Sharlot was forty-two years old, her mother, after a lifetime of illness, died from what appeared to be a culmination of medical difficulties. Without her mother's support and companionship, Sharlot felt a depth of isolation worse than anything she had ever experienced before. Her father's distrust of educated people had left their relationship over the years a tenuous one in which her mother acted as a buffer between their alien personalities. And so father and daughter settled into an uneasy association at the ranch.

James Hall on his own had never been able to earn more than a bare existence for his family. Age, instead of sharpening his skills, seemed to rob him of what few he had. Over the next thirteen years that remained of his life, Sharlot was obliged to assume the primary responsibility for their livelihood. Racked with back pain aggravated by heavy ranch work, devoid of emotional support from family, she increasingly withdrew from friends and from the emotional anchor of writing. But, with unblinking clarity of vision, Sharlot occasionally would sit down and type on the faithful Blickensderfer anecdotes filled with moments of humor and pathos.

Dealing with an unending assortment of ranch hands provided her with what she liked to call cheap entertainment. There was one ranch hand who had a fear of water and the use of the same for cleanliness. He never drank water. He never bathed from one year to the next, and never washed his hands. He was also tubercular. Whenever Sharlot would complete dozens of jars of preserves from the fruit trees, he would sneak into the kitchen when she was attending to something else and would eat out of the jars with his fingers. She hated this, but felt it was useless to fire him, as the next hired man would probably be worse. Many of the ranch hands available who would consider working in Lonesome Valley were either alcoholics or drug addicts.

She liked looking forward to the wonderful frontier day celebrations at Prescott. The women would get together and sit around on benches visiting, catching up on the births, deaths, things that had happened during the year, waiting for the time when the men would parade to the rodeo grounds. Hollywood-style cowboy clothes were never seen. Instead the men wore fine shirts, ties, dark trousers, well-polished boots and grey-tan Stetsons®. Horses were groomed to a high polish. The skill displayed in riding and roping took her breath away. Thunder-showers were always scheduled as part of the day so that everyone could crowd under the roof of the grandstand for additional breathless gossip.

Once one of the biggest long-horned steers broke from the corral and decided to set himself on the grandstand, since that seemed to be a popular and desired location. Everyone started looking for a way to run and most took to hiding under the stands. Everyone was quick with suggestions about who should be given the responsibility of moving the formidable animal, but no one offered to take on the task. Then one of the ranch-women, impatient with the ineffectual chatter, calmly tucked her baby under her arm, picked up her parasol and went over to the steer while everyone held their breath.

At first all that could be heard were the sounds of swatting punctuated by a firm, no-nonsense "git." Suddenly the steer took to bawling something fierce and, as everyone's heart skipped a beat, they could hear it gallop off the stands and run back to the corral, hiding itself in the farthest corner. Arizona's ranch women were fearless. They often had to be. Yet each of the women, in spite of the man-like job they accomplished on the ranch, would not dare to show up at those frontier day

Sharlot Hall in her copper inaugural gown
(Courtesy Sharlot Hall Museum Archives, Prescott)

celebrations without riding side-saddle and dressed in long riding habits of blue broadcloth or black velvet wearing as much trim and frills as they could muster.

During those years on the ranch it appeared as if Sharlot's life of adventuring was over. Her future seemed to be stretching out before her as one made up mostly of isolation and monotony.

Then the unforeseen occurred. Ex-governor Thomas Campbell came to the ranch one day in a totally unexpected visit. The Republicans wanted to place Sharlot's name on the Republican ticket as one of the electors for the Presidential election of Calvin Coolidge. Sharlot was flattered. The idea of a trip to Washington, D.C. awakened in her the excitement she used to feel for traveling. Here was a chance to meet the President of the United States.

On January 18, 1925, she took the train to Washington. Missing from her baggage was a gown that was still in the process of being made for her by a copper company. It was being fashioned out of copper mesh, unique and beautiful, and Sharlot was to wear it to advertise Arizona's copper wealth. She planned to wear it at the inaugural ceremonies.

Sharlot arrived four days later and was met at the station by Senator Ralph Cameron and his wife. Ida Spaulding Cameron had been a friend of Sharlot's during her brief time at school in Prescott. They proceeded immediately to the Senate Office Building where she met dozens of senators. A little later, she was introduced to President Coolidge, who showed his interest by asking her questions about Arizona. In the afternoon she went to the Senate Chamber and presented the sealed envelope with Arizona's votes. She was the first elector and woman to arrive with her state's votes. When Vice President Albert Cummis reached for her envelope, the newspaper photographers started snapping pictures. The next day Sharlot's picture was in most of the major newspapers around the country.

In the evening, Sharlot attended a reception at the White House and met the President again and also had a chance to meet Mrs. Coolidge. She felt as if she was in a dream as she moved slowly along with the nearly four thousand people who were attending the reception. There she was walking through the rooms of the most famous building in the United States, rooms that had seen so much history in the making. She shook

President Coolidge's hand. She liked the keen humor in his eyes and the quiver of a smile on his lips. He did not seem the cold and grave man some made him out to be.

With Ida Cameron as her hostess, guide, mentor and promoter, the next few weeks found Sharlot the object of considerable attention. She was photographed everywhere she went, entertained in high style at the Congressional Club, the Senate Luncheon Club and the Pen Women's League. At each of these occasions she was asked to speak about Arizona and to read some of her poetry. After its arrival, she often wore her copper mesh gown and matching handbag. She even wore a cunningly contrived hat ornamented with tiny cactus. Sharlot came to boost the possibilities of Arizona and ended up becoming the toast of the town.

The actual inauguration took place on March 4. She was able to view the parade from some windows in the post office. Sharlot was delighted to note that Mrs. Coolidge was wearing an Arizona necklace of silver and turquoise that Sharlot had brought with her as a present from the people of Prescott.

In spite of the whirlwind excitement of her visit, Sharlot, the scholar, did not neglect the opportunity to spend many exceedingly happy days working in the Library of Congress. Here indeed was a library to cheer the heart of any dedicated historian. She devoted her research to finding out more about a beloved Arizona pioneer, Buckey O'Neill. With renewed vigor she began writing an in-depth article about his life.

After the inauguration, Sharlot went to New York and Boston to visit friends. It was her intention to take a long, leisurely trip back to Arizona with stops in Chicago and Kansas to give talks and readings of her poetry. But she received news that her father's health had taken a turn for the worst. She cut short her trip to return and provide him with what comfort she could during the last months of his life. He died in June. Sharlot was fifty-five years old. She wondered if now she was finally free to leave the isolation of the ranch out in Lonesome Valley.

Over the years, Sharlot had managed to get aid from various government agencies and other funds to buy the land and the old log building which had been the territorial governor's house. This had been turned over to the city of Prescott so that it could be made into a museum. But there the funding had stopped and there was not sufficient money to restore the old building, which had fallen into a serious state of neglect. Sharlot had written to several businessmen in an attempt to enlist their help in funding the repair costs, but received little encouragement.

It appeared to her that her dream of a museum was never going to become a reality unless she somehow did it herself. Sharlot then decided to approach the Prescott City Council and request a lifetime lease of the building and land. In return, she would at her own expense restore the mansion and would place her entire collection of artifacts that she had gathered over the last forty years within the created museum.

The City Council granted her the lease as well as free water, electricity, police and fire protection for the rest of her life. She sold the ranch with the intention of moving herself and her ten thousand dollar collection of artifacts into the mansion. But the mansion as it stood was unlivable. The filler between the logs had long disappeared from lack of upkeep and the winds blew inside. The roof did not keep out the rain. In time she was able to repair enough to move her furniture into a bedroom upstairs which also served as a workroom. She displayed her collections on the main floor.

Eventually, after several starts and stops in the restoration process, Sharlot was able to formally open the mansion as a museum to visitors. Arizona's current state historian was the first to sign the visitor's register. All kinds of visitors came to see the exhibits and to meet the fascinating lady who had created the museum. Sharlot even had a visit from the mayor of New York City, Fiorello La Guardia.

In her declining years Sharlot spent her time adding by any means she could to the collection of artifacts. She helped get the remains of that wonderful old pioneer, Pauline Weaver, back to Arizona to be reburied on the grounds. She saved the rosebush that one of the wives of a territorial governor had carefully nurtured and brought out west. She spoke to groups of school children, showing them each of the items in the collection and how they were used by the pioneers. She told them the stories of those early days. She enjoyed watching the eyes of those who were turning her words into pictures, glimpsing a time in the world that was long past.

Sharlot Hall had dared to go against the tide of her times. She endured the criticism of people who judged her way of life harshly. Having a husband, they whispered none too quietly, would have taken care of her back pain. Very few ever knew of her longstanding but discreet relationship with Matt Riordan whom she had met through Charles Lummis. His grown daughters would not countenance a divorce from his long-separated wife. Sharlot always met Matt in out-of-the-way places in California. He was the father she never had, the companion, the friend, the lover.

Then there were those who thought she devoted an excessive amount of time to her parents, who blithely labeled her strange and neurotic. But how could she desert her parents? Her mother, after many bouts of illness and pain, had become addicted to morphine. Her father's progressively helpless physical condition dwindled into spells of mental illness.

Perhaps her poem "Cash-In" best describes the twilight days of her life, her determination to live to the fullest, to drink to the last drop the wine of life, and at times to view life through a cynically-humorous lens.

O, Life is a game of poker,
And I've played it straight to the end;
But the last chip's down on the table
And I'm done with the game, my friend.

The deck was stacked by the Dealer
Before he would let me in
The cards were marked, and I knew it
There was never a chance to win.

But I bluffed the game to the finish -
Till He nodded and called my hand,
Palms empty and crossed—my lips smiling still
I knew the Dealer would understand.[3]

Sharlot Mabridth Hall died on April 9, 1943. She was seventy-two years old.

NOTES

[1] Rudyard Kipling, Letter to Sharlot from Nauhakha, Windam County, Vermont (no date). Sharlot Hall Museum Collection, Item 5, File 1, Document Box 1, SHM, Prescott
[2] Sharlot Hall, *Cactus and Pine, Songs of the Southwest*, Sherman and French, Boston, 1910, page 106. Sharlot Hall Museum Collection, Prescott
[3] Josephine MacKenzie, *Poems of a Ranchwoman*, Sharlot Hall Historical Society, 1953, page 10

Territorial Governor's Mansion, Prescott, Arizona
(Courtesy Sharlot Hall Museum)

BIBLIOGRAPHY

Abbey, Sue, Interview with archivist, Sharlot Hall Museum, Prescott, Arizona, April 1988.

Arizona Republican Newspaper, June 16, 1910, "Gathering Material, Miss Sharlot Hall Will Have a Busy Summer."

Crowe, Rosalie and Tod, Diane, *Arizona Women's Hall of Fame*, Arizona Historical Society Museum Monograph, Phoenix, Arizona, 1985.

Fishbough, William, *Library of Mesmerism and Psychology*, Vol. I, Fowler and Wells, Publisher, New York, 1852.

Genung, Charles B., "My First Year in Arizona," typewritten letter from diary box, Sharlot Hall Museum (no date).

Hall, Sharlot, Letter to Charles Lummis, 1899.

Hall, Sharlot, Typewritten notes on Frontier Days, 1926, Sharlot Hall Museum.

Hall, Sharlot, *Cactus and Pine, Songs of the Southwest*, Sherman and French, Boston, 1910.

Hall, Sharlot, "The Father of Arizona," *The New State Magazine*, Vol. II, No. 10, Phoenix, Arizona, August 1912, pages 6-10.

Hall, Sharlot, *Sharlot Hall on the Arizona Strip*, Northland Press, Flagstaff, Arizona, 1975.

Harte, Brett, *Book of Poems*, James Osgood and Company, Boston, 1871.

Kipling, Rudyard, Letter to Sharlot Hall from Nauhakha, Windam County, Vermont (no date).

MacKenzie, Josephine, *Poems of a Ranchwoman*, Sharlot Hall Historical Society, 1953.

Maxwell, Margaret E., *A Passion for Freedom, The Life of Sharlot Hall*, The University of Arizona Press, Tucson, Arizona, 1982.

The Saga of the Superstition Mountains

As seen from Phoenix some thirty-five miles away, the Superstition Mountains jut out from a flat desert plain. Visible on the horizon, their massive, rugged profile prompts the viewer to wonder what stories these spectacular mountains have to tell.

For years they have acted as a backdrop to some of the most exciting and dramatic treasure tales to come out of Arizona. Thousands of men and women, whether treasure-hunting novices or professionals, have come from all over the world, lured by these stories to hunt for gold. Some people have spent the better part of their lives and much of their money looking for the fabled treasure. Their searching has sometimes ended in death. Others continue to roam the mountains, eternally caught in a hypnotic enchantment, enslaved by the quest, the dream of finding treasure, magnificent fabulous treasure which would open all doors to the fulfillment of every wish.

The author has attempted to put together from the facts, figures and legends, a saga about these fascinating mountains. The records and research show many gaps and conflicting information. Yet the saga, like a series of siren songs, draws one ever closer to those gigantic pilings of perilous rocks, allowing the listener to feel the allure but never, never the danger.

The Thunder God's Mountain

Millions of years ago, Arizona was a low, flat land covered by a huge inland sea. Underneath that beguilingly calm sea was a slowly cooling crust of earth. Cracks developed in that subterranean crust from the pressures of unknown forces. The sea water rushed into the molten interior, creating steam of such magnitude that it began a cataclysmic chain reaction. Lava and volcanic matter spewed up through the sea thousands of feet into the air.

When this fiery volcanic mass cooled, it hardened into a stupefying series of cliffs and peaks, twisting canyons and impenetrable mazes of rocks. In time, the volcanic matter produced such a vast assortment of cacti and thorny shrubs that in places neither man nor beast could pass easily.

Native Americans believed this land was a sacred place. They called it the home of the Thunder God and his people. They knew that in this mountainous area the Thunder God owned a great treasure.

Over four hundred years ago, the famous Spanish explorer, Francisco Coronado, came to this land looking for gold. He wanted the Indians to guide him and his men in their search for this treasure, but the Indians refused. They said that all who trespassed on the sacred land of the Thunder God would be punished. Coronado and his men laughed at the medicine men's stories and started exploring on their own. Soon strange things began to happen. Some of the men fell off cliffs, some broke bones, others simply disappeared.

Coronado's party of explorers grew fearful. It was eerie the way the storm clouds always gathered there. Never had they witnessed such violent rainstorms! The name he decided to give the place reflected their emerging fear. He called the place *Monte Superstition*. That is how the Superstition Mountains came to be named.

For the next three hundred years, these mountains stood in solitude, revered only for their sacred splendor. Then in the early 1840s, on a Sonoran cattle rancho owned by the wealthy, arrogant Don Miguel Peralta, a series of events would once again bring the Superstition Mountains into prominence.

Don Miguel had the reputation of being a capricious, selfish man. He was virtually an absolute ruler of his cattle kingdom as well as dictator of the five hundred people who worked under him.

Although Don Miguel had three sons, Pedro, Ramon and the young Miguel, his only interest outside of himself was his beautiful daughter, Rosita Maria. Men for miles around the rancho were bewitched by her breathtaking beauty and fell madly in love with her. But Rosita Maria, used to constant attention and having her own way, was spoiled and soon became bored with them all. Only Carlos, handsome, aloof, exceedingly polite Carlos, piqued her curiosity.

Here, thought Rosita Maria, was a man who did not fawn. Here was a challenge, perhaps a man worthy of her. If Carlos thought that he could remain immune to her charms, he did not understand that she was her father's daughter. She was as determined to succeed in the business of love as was her father in the business of cattle ranching. Her provocative lips hardened with resolve. It will only be a matter of time, she thought, before Carlos, too, becomes my slave, just like all the others.

Meanwhile, Don Miguel, sharp-eyed and brilliant in his handling of his successful cattle rancho, was like a blind man to his daughter's activities. Then late one moonlit night, the guard posted as watchman sounded the alarm. Instantly everyone in the Peralta village was aroused. In seconds the men had all grabbed weapons and rushed to the hacienda prepared to defend the rancho. Questions of concern were on the lips of everyone. Were cattle being stolen? Were horses being taken? Were the storehouses being broken into?

What Don Miguel and his assembled men saw was the beautiful Rosita Maria running toward her father's hacienda, screaming hysterically. In the shimmering light of the moon, they could see that she was completely nude.

"*Madre de Dios, mi hija*, my daughter," cried Don Miguel as he flung his cape over his daughter's trembling shoulders.

"*Papa, Papito,*" Rosita Maria sobbed, "it was Carlos. Carlos did this to me."

In those few emotional moments, Don Miguel failed to see the young Carlos quietly lead a horse from the corral, mount it and dash away. The clatter of the horse's hooves finally distracted everyone's attention from the sobbing Rosita Maria, as the entire village and Don Miguel stood stunned listening to the escaping Carlos.

Don Miguel's face contorted with anger. "Move, you idiots," he bellowed, "bring him to me. I will kill him with my bare hands."

Immediately the men started after Carlos, but in the darkness of the night, it soon became apparent that they would not find him without the help of Indian guides. Returning to the rancho, they explained to Don Miguel their need for Indian trackers. It did not take long for two Indian guides to be found.

When Wolf Nose and his companion were brought before Don Miguel, they said, "We will find him. We do not need the others. Lend us two swift horses and we will do the rest." Don

The mysterious Superstition Mountains
(Courtesy Arizona Office of Tourism)

Miguel gave them what they wanted.

Early the next morning the sounds of hammering broke the pre-dawn stillness as the profile of a gallows was silhouetted against the rising sun. Rosita Maria, awakened by the sounds of activity, came out of the hacienda. Seemingly recovered from the night before, she examined the wooden platform as she walked around it. Two women servants rushed to her side, beseeching her to return to the protection of the house. But Rosita Maria haughtily refused. She continued to stand in front of the hacienda as more of the people of the rancho gathered around to watch. Observing the whispered conversations and the significant glances in her direction, she called arrogantly to her father, amused by the sensation she was creating, "Will you hang Carlos, *Padre mio?*"

For the first time in her life, her father turned on her— scowling. "His feet will be tied to the floor of the scaffold," he said. "His hands will be attached to a rope thrown over the bar. A basket will be hung from the other end of the rope. Rocks, heavy rocks, will be put into the basket to lower it each hour." He snarled, "In two days, something will break."

So, thought Rosita Maria with an indifferent sigh, this was how her romantic episode with Carlos would end.

For the next week, Don Miguel stormed and raged, demanding to know why the two Indian trackers had not returned. Impatiently, he waited another week. Not a word, not a message, nothing arrived from the two Indians. Then early one afternoon, Wolf Nose staggered into the rancho alone, without his companion or his horse. He was starving, thirsty and exhausted.

"Speak, you dog," thundered Don Miguel, "why have you come back empty-handed?"

Unable to speak, Wolf Nose pulled out a pouch from under the skin of his loincloth. He opened the pouch and allowed the contents to fall into his hands. Before Don Miguel's eyes was a small pile of the richest gold nuggets he had ever seen. One of the nuggets was the size of a walnut.

Taking the gold, Don Miguel fingered it thoughtfully. "Feed him, give him water," he commanded, "allow him some rest. Tonight," he said to the Indian, "tonight you will tell me everything that happened."

That evening Wolf Nose told of how he and his companion had carefully tracked Carlos, each day getting a little closer. Then, one morning, they saw Carlos galloping toward them. They grabbed their guns.

"Don't shoot," cried the young man. "Look, I have gold, much gold, there is much gold, there is lots more where this came from." Surprised by this unexpected turn of events, the Indians paused to consider the young Carlos. His face was suffused with an uncontrollable excitement. He continued to speak, "I could not help myself. I tried to ignore her, but she taunted me with her flashing eyes and her sweet-smelling hair. I became like a wild man. But gold, with lots of gold I will come back. I will persuade Don Miguel to let me marry my beautiful Rosita Maria. If he will allow me to have her, I will make him a fabulously rich man." Even Wolf Nose knew that if a man had enough gold and the promise of more, he could buy immunity from almost any punishment.

The Indians went with Carlos to the source of the gold deep

within the country of the Thunder God. Filling their saddle bags from a vein found hidden in a recess in the ground, they marked their location by a nearby peak of reddish rock and then began the long journey back to the rancho.

After journeying for two days, they came to a river which was often dry, but now was a swollen, rushing torrent of water. The Indians said that they would have to wait for at least a day for the water to subside. But Carlos was impatient, anxious not to delay.

"We can do it," he said. "We can swim our horses across—I know we can." The Indians reluctantly followed Carlos into the river. They were soon engulfed by the raging, churning water. Only Wolf Nose was able to survive by clinging to a branch of a cottonwood tree. The only gold that remained was in the small pouch he had tucked into the waist of his loincloth. With the horses dead, he was forced to walk without food or water back to the Peralta rancho.

During the next three years, Don Miguel went with his sons on mining expeditions to the land of the Thunder People. Because the surrounding area contained much high-grade gold concentrate, they made several other mining shafts besides the primary one which held the vein of gold. Don Miguel was always able to remember exactly where the mine was located by a landmark, a peculiarly-shaped peak that looked to him like the pointed top of a sombrero hat. Secretly, over the next three years, Don Miguel took millions of pesos worth of pure gold concentrate from the mining shafts of his Sombrero Mine.

But Mexico, without realizing what treasure had been discovered on its territory, signed in 1848 the Treaty of Guadalupe-Hidalgo and accepted, seven years later, the terms of the Gadsden Purchase. The Peralta Mine was now a part of the United States.

Don Miguel decided to make one final trip to his Sombrero Mine, leaving his sons behind in charge of the rancho. This time, he decided, he would take four hundred men and as many mules and burros. This time he would take out billions of pesos of gold.

But the Apaches were angry about these Mexicans coming and defiling the sacred land of their Thunder God. If that was not insulting enough, the Mexican miners made merry with the

Apache maidens who were fascinated with these amusing, singing, guitar-strumming men from the South.

The Apache leaders, Mangas Coloradas and Cochise, joined forces and brought together a large contingent of warriors, with the intent of attacking Peralta.

Don Miguel, learning of their plan, quickly stopped operating the mine. His men covered and hid the shaft openings as best they could and made preparations to depart. While this was being done, Don Miguel drew a map of the location and carved out hieroglyphics on some rocks as a key to the map. With all evidence of his activity in the area concealed, Don Miguel withdrew his miners and equipment to a mesa, high in the Superstitions. There he planned to load all the burros and mules with all the gold concentrate that they could carry. During the night they would steal away from the three-thousand-foot mesa and make a run for the rancho.

But Coloradas and Cochise learned of Don Miguel's plan and quietly placed their warriors along the canyon and cliffs of the escape route. The Mexicans never had a chance. They were taken completely by surprise and at a disadvantage with the heavily-laden mules and burros. The pack animals stampeded, frightening the horses of Don Miguel's guards.

It was a massacre. No one survived. The Apaches dumped much of the gold concentrate, not recognizing the ore in its unrefined form. They added further camouflage to hide the mine shafts except for one which they felt was in such a rugged place no one would ever find it. Some of the pack animals escaped to wander the twisting canyons with their precious gold until they perished from old age or accident.

And so the story of the massacre and the treasure of gold began to be whispered about from village to village in Sonora. The story fueled the fantasies of a poor people who dreamed of how such wealth could change their lives.

Several years later, a squad from the United States Army came across the bloody scene and gathered up what was left of the bodies and gave them a burial in a large common grave. Don Miguel's body was never found. The journal records do not indicate whether the army ever found any of the gold concentrate.

Now the story was whispered about at the forts, saloons and

Superstition Mountains, thirty miles east of Phoenix
(Courtesy Arizona Office of Tourism, Phoenix)

towns of Arizona. More and more men turned a speculative eye toward those distinctive-looking mountains.

And so *Monte Superstition,* created with such volcanic upheaval, echoed anew with another kind of violence, the violence of greedy men.

Two Mexican War Veterans

Even as far back as the mid-1800s, people often said that the exploits of Don Peralta were nothing but a legend, a tale for telling around the campfire. Perhaps, but many people also believed the legends might be based on truth. After all, there was a Don Miguel Peralta and there is substantiating evidence supporting the fact that he had worked a mine of value.

Because of the strength of the legend, the Superstition Mountains attracted a great many gold seekers. All kinds of people came, unable to resist the lure of gold, hoping against hope that they would find the illusive Peralta mine.

Sometime after 1848, at the end of the Mexican-American War, two army veterans, down on their luck, came to the Superstitions to look for the Peralta gold. Sean O'Connor and Aloysious Hurley were prospecting near the Superstitions when they found the skeleton of a burro and part of a disintegrated packsaddle. The saddlebag contained a strange-colored rock, which they immediately recognized as gold concentrate of great worth. In subsequent weeks, they found the decayed remains of several other mules. In each instance, a dusty saddlebag lay nearby filled with gold.

These two former sons of Ireland eventually sold the contents of the bags to the San Francisco mint. Gold was worth approximately $13 an ounce and the two men received a total of $37,000 for their find. During those days, an average yearly income was well under a thousand dollars. By the standards of the time, they had become rich men.

Hurley and O'Connor returned to the Superstitions for several years and continued to find an occasional skeleton and a decaying saddlebag filled with its precious ore. Although the men tried to keep their finds a secret, somehow the information leaked out. Now, not only did they have to deal with the treacherous and rugged terrain of the mountains, but they soon began to meet up with robbers and riffraff determined to follow and kill the men for their gold. They began to realize that their lives were increasingly at risk. The Superstitions teemed with this amoral element as well as with angry Indians resenting the continued trespass by white men. Hurley and O'Connor moved to Idaho where they lived in comfort and regaled many with their story of the Superstition Mountains.

For years the very existence of a Peralta mine had been questioned; now speculation focused on its whereabouts. Some argued that the mine was located in the Superstition Mountains; others believed it was in the Goldfield area adjacent to the Superstitions. Still others claimed that Peralta's mine was in Yavapai County near Bumble Bee. Not only does the story told by Hurley and O'Connor give credence to the Peralta massacre, it goes further in suggesting a general location for the fabled mine.

A Doctor Comes to Fort McDowell

There was yet another individual who profited from the lost Peralta saddlebags. In 1865, a young army doctor named Abraham Thorne received his first appointment to the newly-established Fort McDowell. Thorne's responsibility was to provide the settlers with medical aid. The military was needed in this area because of continuing harrassment from hostile Indians. Fort McDowell also gave sanctuary to those peaceful Indians who detested the constant fighting. These Indians lived in a nearby area and were provided with some means for survival.

Originally from Illinois, the young doctor was completely fascinated by everything he saw in Arizona. A sense of adventure permeated every aspect of life on the frontier. Thorne found his work at the fort to be both challenging and rewarding.

Once he had seen to the immediate medical needs of the settlers and soldiers, he decided to use his spare time to give what medical help he could to the peaceful Indians living nearby. What he saw disturbed him. These natives were living in neglect and squalor. Accustomed to a transient life on large tracts of land, the Indians had never developed a basic understanding of the sanitation needs necessary for those who remain in a specific and confined area. Disease was rampant and everywhere he turned young Thorne saw the results of what happens to people who do not have knowledge of even the simplest basic health habits.

Thorne tried to communicate with the Indians and to share his medical expertise. He found himself being rebuffed from fear. Their experiences with the white man had never been good. Determined to help in whatever way he could, he began to teach himself their language and to slowly win their trust.

He taught the women how to care for their children in such a way as to avoid a devastating eye disease that prevailed in the camp. He showed the midwives techniques to help during a difficult birth. He cleverly included the medicine men in his teaching program, showing them how to set broken bones and use simple medicines. Eventually the medicine men took over the responsibility of policing the camp and teaching the new arrivals the ways to keep the camp sanitary and disease-free.

The Indians were amazed with his healing ways and his facility in learning their language. Here was a white man like no other. In a rare gesture of acceptance, they began to call him their brother.

Then one day, while at the Indian camp, Doctor Thorne was approached by a man he had never seen before. The tall, aristocratic Indian had a manner that reflected the ease of one who is a leader. The famous Indian chief, Cochise, had come in person to the young doctor. His youngest wife was experiencing a difficult pregnancy and birth. Would the healer of so many of his brothers come and see his wife?

Dr. Abraham Thorne was able to successfully help the beautiful young wife of Cochise through the pregnancy. The great chief was overjoyed and promised to never forget the kind healing of this young, dedicated man.

Eventually the doctor was given orders to go to another assignment in New Mexico. When the Indians learned that their white medicine man would be leaving them, they were very sad. They asked for a gathering of their chiefs, Geronimo and Cochise, as well as their wisemen. They wanted to somehow thank him for helping their people.

Dr. Thorne was summoned to appear before their leaders. He was told that because he had helped their people, it was their wish to give him a gift. If he would be willing to wait for one night and one day they would take him to a place where there was much gold.

At the agreed time, Dr. Thorne was blindfolded and taken over a long and circuitous route. When they finally stopped, and the doctor's blindfold was taken off, he saw that they were in a narrow canyon. The Indians waved to a large pile of rocks directly in front of him. The rock was of a curious color. Thorne dismounted and picked up a small chunk of the ore and realized with stunned disbelief that the Indians were giving him a fortune in gold.

Thorne was blindfolded again for the trip out, so he was never certain where the Indians had taken him. The Indians said they wanted to protect him from their powerful god and from greedy ones who might come to seek such treasure. Just once on the return trip did the Indians take the blindfold off. It was to allow Thorne the opportunity for a drink of water. He immediately saw that he was in a much larger canyon. When he looked in the distance, he saw rising against the sky an immense spire of rock which he recognized as that unusually-shaped peak called Weaver's Needle.

Before going to his new post in New Mexico, Doctor Thorne requested permission to visit some of his family living near San Francisco. While in the city, he exchanged his gold at the mint for an undisclosed sum of money. The amount must have been considerable because he generously paid off a loan his father owed on a business venture and then gave his two brothers sufficient funds for each to build a substantial home. When questioned about the source of his new-found wealth, he spoke vaguely of a bit of luck that had come his way during his stay at Fort McDowell.

Years later, still a considerably wealthy man, he shared his story with his family and thus added one further tale to the ever-increasing saga of the Superstition Mountains.

The Lost Dutchman Gold Mine

Treasure ignites the imagination, and imagination fuels its own fire. Amidst the hundreds of treasure stories in the world, the following one intrigues, puzzles and continues to fascinate.

The story starts with a misconception, that the Dutchman was from Holland. In fact he was a Deutscheman, a native of Germany. His name was Jacob Waltz. Well over six feet tall, Jacob was a physically imposing man with the bearing of a Prussian soldier.

Educated as a mining engineer, he could not resist the lure of the California gold rush of 1848 and came to the United States with dreams of striking it rich. Success in California, however, eluded him and in the early 1860s Jacob arrived in Arizona as a prospector. There is a recorded mining claim of Waltz's filed in the Walker Mining District near Prescott. Like so many others who sought after the elusive dream of gold, Jacob's claim brought little reward.

In 1863, a discouraged Jacob Waltz hired on as an ordinary miner at one of the most famous gold mines in Arizona, the Vulture Mine, located near Wickenburg. While employed at the mine, Jacob saw the dream of striking it rich come to life, as millions of dollars of gold were extracted for the benefit of the owners. Envious, some of the hired hands also began removing gold illegally for their own gain. "High-grading" ore in their lunch pails, in the cuffs of their trousers, and in their pockets, they removed unknown amounts. In the early days of mining at the Vulture, when excitement was running high about the quality and quantity of the ore being mined, the owners did not realize how much gold was being "high-graded." Some of the miners were becoming very rich men.

Astute in the ways of the world, Jacob Waltz realized what was happening at the mine, but his attention was diverted elsewhere. While living in the mining camp, he had met and fallen in love with a lovely young Apache girl named Ken-Tee. This growing relationship was frowned upon by the local inhabitants, who disapproved of any form of serious fraternization between a white man and an Indian woman. In fact, marriage to a native American was against the law. But the attraction between this austere Deutscheman and this nature-loving Indian woman remained strong.

The owners of the Vulture eventually began to realize the extent of the "high-grading" being practiced. Jacob Waltz and several other miners found themselves accused and threatened with legal repercussions. Living quarters and belongings were searched. One hundred seventy-five thousand dollars in gold was found. The miners caught with gold in their possession were arrested for theft. Jacob Waltz and several others were suspected of being a part of this theft, but no solid proof was ever found to back up this belief. Nonetheless they were fired and told to get out of Wickenburg, and stay out.

Jacob and Ken-Tee moved southeast to an area near Mesa about 13 miles from the Superstition Mountains. There they built themselves a home. The neighbors, few and widely scattered, paid little attention to the newly arrived couple. Life took on a rhythmic flow of contentment.

While living in Mesa, Waltz met another German prospector, Jacob Weiser. The two men soon became good friends and often would go into the mountains prospecting for gold. They knew that somewhere out in the vast expanses of Arizona, there were riches to be found and they wanted to be the ones to find it. For several years Jacob settled into a routine of companionship

Weaver's Needle in the distance (Courtesy Arizona Historical Foundation, Hayden Library, Arizona State University, Tempe)

with Ken-Tee and episodic adventures searching for gold with his countryman, Weiser.

On one occasion, the two men were prospecting in the mountains near Nogales, Mexico. They heard about a fiesta which was taking place in the neighboring town of Arizpa. Intrigued with the bustle and activities of the festival, the two Jacobs decided to go for a drink in the local saloon. There they watched a card game which was in progress. One of the players was the son of Don Miguel Peralta, the fabled Mexican cattle rancher.

Waltz and Weiser soon noticed that the card dealer was cheating and informed the young Miguel Peralta. Miguel, angry that the card game was rigged, accused the dealer, who vehemently denied everything. The argument escalated into a gunfight, leaving the card dealer dead, young Miguel shot in the chest, and Weiser wounded with a bullet in his arm.

Weiser and Waltz immediately found medical help for Miguel, thereby saving his life. In order to repay the two men, young Miguel invited them to the Peralta hacienda and during their visit told them about his father's mine, which was now a part of the United States. He then offered them a proposition. If the two prospectors would become his partners, he would show them where the mine was located. As Americans, they could lay claim to it, mine it and then all three of them could share in the profits.

A party was outfitted and the three men traveled north to the Superstitions. Miguel remembered the location of only one entrance to the mine. When they reached that shaft, they proceeded to extract about $30,000 in gold.

Taking his share, young Miguel returned to Mexico. Waltz and Weiser continued working the mine for some time. Waltz often returned to Mesa to be with Ken-Tee and to get more supplies. On one trip, Waltz stayed a little longer than usual. When he returned, he found Weiser's dead body pierced by a dozen arrows. Waltz hurriedly buried his partner and returned to Mesa, fearful of another Apache attack.

But it was already too late. The Apaches were watching and followed Waltz. When they saw that he was living with Ken-Tee, the Indians became convinced that it was she who had shown the location of their sacred treasure to the white man. Outraged that one of their own people had betrayed their Thunder God, they planned revenge. During the early morning hours, they raided Waltz's house and carried off Ken-Tee.

Waltz and a group of neighbors quickly followed in pursuit. The raiding Apaches were attacked and during the fight they released Ken-Tee. Waltz leaped off his horse, rushed to the fallen Ken-Tee and cradled her in his arms. "My darling, my treasure, what has happened?" The young woman raised her hand to Jacob's craggy face, and opened her mouth to speak, but only blood gushed out. The Indians had made certain that she would never speak again. As Jacob held Ken-Tee in his arms, her life slowly slipped away.

Waltz was utterly devastated, not only by the death of his beloved Ken-Tee, but also by the death of his best friend and partner, Weiser. In the aftermath of his grief, he became a secretive loner who often took to drink. Unable to bear the memories that haunted his home in Mesa, he moved to a house in Phoenix near Buckeye Road and Seventh Street.

From that time on, he would occasionally venture out from Phoenix, disappear for several weeks and come back with large quantities of gold ore. Waltz would then take his ore to the local Wells Fargo office and ship it to the United States Mint in San Francisco. In due time, he would receive thousands of dollars in return. In the excitement of the moment, Waltz would spend some of his money in the local saloons and become roaring drunk. Sometimes he would brag about knowing where there was enough gold to pave every street in Phoenix.

Jacob Waltz became a figure of speculation and fascination in Phoenix. Between 1870 and 1880, word of his drunken mutterings began to spread. People gossiped about a man living in Arizona, called "the old Dutchman," who had discovered a gold mine so rich that he could go to it and pick up a sack of almost pure gold anytime he wanted. Attempting to discover the source of his treasure, people tried to curry his favor. Others took to spying on him, following him wherever he went. Viewed as an eccentric local celebrity, reporters and writers tried to interview him.

But, Jacob Waltz rebuffed all advances. Suspicious of everyone, and jaded by the calculating glitter in the eyes of strangers who pretended friendship, he remained a loner. There was only one thing that he did participate in: shooting contests. Perhaps he hoped that his prowess with a rifle would discourage those who might want to kidnap him and force him to reveal his secret. All the while his reputation continued to grow. Did he ever feel like a fledgling mockingbird surrounded by greedy cats?

In February 1891 the old Dutchman's luck finally ran out. A disastrous one-hundred-year-flood struck, devastating Phoenix. Situated near the north bank of the Salt River, Waltz's house was caught in a sudden onslaught of water. He was forced to climb a tall cottonwood tree which stood near his home. Eighty-three years old, Waltz lashed himself to the tree, knowing that lack of sleep or fatigue would cause him to lose his grip, plunging him into the swirling waters.

Two days later, he was sighted, rescued and taken to the home of Mrs. Julia Thomas, who owned a boarding house and confectionery store. But, the exposure had caused him to contract pneumonia, at that time a death-causing disease. The old Dutchman hung onto life, fighting as best he could. He died several months later.

Jacob Waltz was barely laid in his grave, when a rumor started that during his last moments, as a gesture of gratitude to Mrs. Thomas, he had revealed to her the whereabouts of his mine.

Mrs. Thomas' actions certainly suggest that something important had transpired just before his death. With no explanation to anyone, Mrs. Thomas sold her store and, taking with her a 17-year-old boarder, Rhinehart Petrasch, she set out for the Superstition Mountains. After some months of searching, she appealed to Rhinehart's father and brother, who were experienced prospectors, to join them. The search continued for another year before it was abandoned.

Many years later, when Mrs. Thomas was quite old, she revealed to Jim Bark, a prominent Arizona rancher, the information Jacob Waltz had told her. "Waltz told me," she said, "that the mouth of the mine could be found on a spot upon which the shadow of the tip of Weaver's Needle, that well-known peak, rests at exactly four in the afternoon.

"Mr. Bark, the directions seemed simple enough," said Julia, "until you realize that the sun's shadow moves every single day throughout the year. But, we followed that shadow, we carefully searched the surrounding area. The only thing we found was a trench dug on a claim near Goldfield, but never a mine. I believed him," said Mrs. Thomas. "It sounded so real. He said that the mine had a ledge of rose quartz with an additional few inches of crystal hematite. How could he have made this description up?" she muttered to herself. "One-third of those few inches was gold, and the rose quartz was generously sprinkled with pinhead-size lumps of gold. He told me that it was a king's treasure waiting, waiting for someone to discover."

Julia Thomas laughed bitterly. She had lost her boarding house and her store believing the old Dutchman's story. "I think now he made it all up because he couldn't pay me at the end. But he had gold. We all knew he had some gold—he lived on it for years. All I know is that he made it sound so very, very real."

Beginning with a misconception, does the story also end with a misconception? The old Dutchman's tale continues to be repeated throughout Arizona and throughout the country. It leaves more questions than it ever answered. Was there a mine? Was it the fabled Peralta mine? Why did Jacob Waltz never exploit his mine, return to Germany and flaunt the wealth he claimed was his?

Charles Hall and the Peralta Legacy

Around the turn of the century, a mining prospector from Denver came to Prescott to work. Charles Hall decided that while he was in Arizona he would look around for mining possibilities and check out the Superstition area. He was particularly interested in Goldfield Hill, which was not far from the site of the Peralta massacre. As he looked over the terrain, Hall began to question the part of the story that suggested Peralta had retreated to this mesa. Closely examining the type of rock on the mesa, he began to suspect that Peralta had in fact mined from the mesa itself. Charles Hall decided to try out his theory. He bought the mining claims to Goldfield Hill from some Mormon owners, and then put together a mining operation.

Hall decided to sink his first shaft directly down the center of the hill. What he found was high-grade gold concentrate. During the next few years, Charles Hall took out millions of dollars of gold from his Mammoth Mine. It now appeared that this man had finally found the elusive gold of Don Miguel Peralta and Jacob Waltz. The search was over, the puzzling questions resolved.

But what of the Indian belief that this sacred land of their Thunder God would punish all who trespassed? One day, after several years of successful mining, black thunder clouds began to build up and lightning flashed ominously over the mountains. At first Charles Hall was not alarmed; the area was known for its thunder clouds. Then the rains came like a river of water pouring off the mountains, joining together in an ever-increasing force. This also did not appear to be unusual. But the rains did not diminish, instead they became worse. An awesome flood of torrential waters crashed over the Mammoth Mine's site. Machinery was smashed and thousands of tons of sand and earth completely filled the shafts, burying everything.

Hall, who was quite old by the time of this exceptional storm, made no further effort to resurrect the mine. Perhaps he finally believed the medicine men's warnings. Perhaps he was just tired of adding more to his millions in wealth.

When he died, his daughters sold his holdings to George Young, a former mayor of Phoenix. Young sank a probe shaft down into the mesa, only to find an underground river of such pressure that in spite of the use of pumps working day and night, Young was unable to eliminate the underground water. The Mammoth Mine was finished.

Not everyone believed that the Mammoth Mine fully explained Jacob Waltz's description to Julia as to how the gold was formed. These people wondered if there was yet another shaft, another mine still undiscovered.

A Final Discovery

One day, not too many years ago, a man named Alfred Strong Lewis went to visit a business friend of his who lived in the Superstition Mountains area. Al Lewis was so excited he could hardly form his words in coherent sentences. "I know it sounds crazy, after all this while, but I think, I just think I've found the old Dutchman's mine."

His friend, Ted Sliger, just smiled and said, "Hey, slow down Al, don't tell me you've finally fallen for that old story."

Al Lewis paid little attention to his friend, continuing to speak almost as if to himself. "I was exploring in an area just a short way from the northwest part of the Superstitions and no more than a mile from where the Peralta massacre occurred. That's when I saw this large boulder. When I examined the boulder closely, I noticed what looked like a mysterious little entrance right under it. At first I thought I was mistaken.

Sometimes things look contrived when in fact they are just a natural phenomenon. Anyway, I explored further and I found the remains of a neatly-dug passage. I decided to get me a few sticks of dynamite and topple the boulder. Ted, I found a shaft made of old timbers of ironwood. The wood was fashioned the way the Spaniards used to work ironwood over one hundred years ago. It looks like it might be an old Peralta mine shaft."

By this time Ted Sliger had stopped smiling in an amused fashion, every ounce of his attention riveted on his friend. Al Lewis continued speaking, "I have a chance to buy the mineral claim for the area, but I don't have enough money, can you help me?" Ted Sliger not only agreed to help Al, but contacted two wealthy business friends of his to also join in helping Al Lewis gain possession of the claim.

Later that night, the four men contacted the owner of the property and bought the mining rights for $20,000, backing the agreement with a $5,000 deposit.

When the men began to explore the shaft, they could see where someone had broken off chunks of ore which contained a high percentage of free gold. Everything seemed to point to this being not only one of the Peralta shafts, but also Jacob Waltz's lost mine.

The four associates began to take ore out of the shaft as fast as they could, amassing about $42,000 in gold. Then the shaft abruptly stopped. They decided to continue the shaft further; when they started to expand it, they broke through a wall of rock and found themselves in what appeared to be another abandoned shaft. This one was of a much more modern construction. It appeared to be a branch of the Mammoth Mine's mining shaft.

Exploring this shaft as far as they could, they discovered that some sort of landslide had cut off the vein. The flooding of the Mammoth Mine seemed to have mixed up everything underground. The vein seemed to be gone, lost, broken and churned up in some sort of cataclysmic episode. The men brought some large dirt-moving machinery and began scraping and digging the surface around the two shafts. There was gold in every foot of the ground, enough to pay for costs, but not enough to make a profit. The men continued to move enormous amounts of earth in hopes of hitting the lost vein. Eventually they gave up.

To work for costs alone was not enough.

What do geologists say about all these stories coming out of the Superstition Mountains area? Geologists tell us that the Superstitions themselves developed earlier than the age of mineralization. Weaver's Needle is a volcanic plug composed mostly of basaltic rock which is not the right kind of rock for mineral ores. Could there be any circumstance which might cause some sort of mineralization in a volcanic area? It would have to be a rare kind of circumstance, they always answer. Occasionally, during a volcanic episode, a chimney vent is formed to allow for escaping gas. Later, during the cooling down period, the rock vent can become filled with minerals normally foreign to the area. Could that elusive vein of gold be a product of such a vent?

The saga of the Superstitions never seems to lose its ability to fascinate. Periodically a new book or a new magazine article will be published and a new rash of speculation will begin again, a new set of questions will be asked. Will the sacred home of the Thunder God ever reveal all of its secrets? Will new dreamers of great treasure continue to search for that tantalizing vein of quartz with its filings of pure gold?

BIBLIOGRAPHY

Allen, Robert Joseph, *The Story of Superstition Mountain and The Lost Dutchman Gold Mine*, Pocket Books, Simon and Schuster, Inc., 1971.

Arnold, Oren, *Ghost Gold*, Revised Edition, The Naylor Company, 1971.

Black, Harry G., *The Lost Dutchman Mine*, Branden Press, Boston, 1975.

Cook, James E., "Pima Teachings Give Superstition Mountains Sacred Context," *The Arizona Republic*, Thursday, December 29, 1988.

Jennings, Gary, *The Treasure of the Superstition Mountains*, W. W. Norton & Company, New York, 1973.

Lee, Robert E., *The Lost Dutchman Mine*, Dick Martin Co. Inc., San Diego, California, 1976.

Mitchell, John D., *Lost Mines of the Great Southwest*, The Rio Grande Press, Inc., New Mexico, 1970.

Storm, Barry, *Gold of the Superstitions*, The Southwestern Press, Phoenix, 1940.

Trimble, Marshall, *Arizona Adventure*, Golden West Publishers, Arizona, 1982.

Our Heroine Was No Lady

Circumstances can create a person's destiny. It changed the pathway of one of Arizona's earliest pioneer women, Sarah Bowman.

Sarah was born in Clay County, Missouri, in 1812. Life in Missouri in those days was a primitive existence. Sarah, had she taken the usual path of her sex, would have lived an isolated life on a frontier farm. Dressed in worn faded gingham, with little chance of receiving even a rudimentary education, she would have married as a young teenager and produced child after child on a yearly basis. She would have lived out her life in the confines of her homestead with little opportunity of ever seeing any other part of the world besides the region where she lived.

But for Sarah Bowman, circumstance was to dictate otherwise. By the time Sarah was seventeen years old, she had grown to over six feet. In 1829, the average man was approximately five feet five inches, and women were of even smaller dimensions. A life of anonymity was not to be the fate of any young woman whose well-proportioned figure rose to the startling height of six feet two inches. Yet, nature seemed determined to add even more: her head was crowned with an abundant halo of burnished copper-colored hair.

Sarah observed the life around her in Missouri and knew she was meant for bigger and better things. As a young woman, she married Adolfus Aue, who dreamed of the adventure and excitement of a military life. She insisted on joining him, becoming a laundress and cook for the army during the Seminole War in Florida. Her new life agreed with her. She liked the free, easy ways of the military. She reveled in the company of men, enjoying their masculine attention. She welcomed her new life as a thirsty animal welcomes the rain.

The records tell us only that Sarah lost her first husband. She also had children, but nothing is known of them. As a camp follower, there was no real place for children in the military life, so she very probably farmed them out to relatives and friends.

By 1846, Sarah, now in her thirties, was in Texas following General Zachary Taylor's army as it prepared to engage in the Mexican War. She was married once again, this time to a

Charles Bourgette of the Fifth Infantry.

Zack Taylor moved his relatively small army of mostly volunteers across the southern coast to Texas. When they arrived at an arroyo of the Colorado River, they discovered the Mexicans lined up on the other side. A messenger from the Mexican commandant informed General Taylor that, if he crossed the river, he would be fired upon.

Sarah, indignant with the Mexicans, was heard to tell some of the soldiers that if the general would give her a sturdy pair of trousers (they were called tongs in those days), she would personally wade across the river and whip every Mexican scoundrel who showed his face. The men cheered. If their Sarah, who was nicknamed "the Great Western" after the largest steam ship in the United States at that time, was not afraid, why should they be?

General Taylor was not easily bluffed. The men crossed without drawing fire. When the army reached the Rio Grande River, they began to build a fort nearby which they named Fort Texas. Later the name was changed to Fort Brown.

Taylor, a hard-nosed military man, was worried about the security of his supply line route. Taking part of his army, which included Sarah's husband, he marched to the coast to strengthen the line. The general left the women and the Seventh Infantry to maintain and guard the fort.

The Mexicans, recognizing the vulnerability of Fort Brown, began to bombard it from across the river. The women were ordered to retreat to the relative safety of some nearby empty magazines, where arms and ammunition were normally stored. They were ordered to sew sandbags from the canvas of the officers' tents.

Sarah refused to sew. She refused to go with the other women to the protection of the magazines. If their men were out there being fired upon, the least someone could do was feed them. She set up a kitchen in the middle of the fort. Throughout the bombardment, she made certain that there was always coffee for the men and, with what meager supplies she had, she made them tasty meals.

Stray bullets came close: one went through her bonnet, one hit a tray of coffee that she was carrying. But, in spite of the palpable danger, Sarah remained cheerful. She helped care for the wounded. She had made up her mind that no one was going to endure all that danger without a helping hand, a hot meal, or some consoling nursing.

Six days of sitting in this hell of bombardment abruptly stopped when Taylor returned with the remainder of his forces. By this time, Sarah was not only known as the Great Western, she was now also the heroine of Fort Brown. The price of her new fame was high; she had become a widow. Charles Bourgette had been killed securing General Taylor's supply line.

The United States Army moved south of the Rio Grande to the town of Saltillo, located in the central mountains of Mexico. There Sarah set up the American House for the soldiers. It was a meeting place, boarding house, a place to leave letters, notes, messages and a place to socialize. Sarah also set about the task of learning Spanish so she could converse with the Mexicans hired to help her. She soon became quite proficient in the language.

Sarah always cared about the needs of the men, all their needs. She had a group of willing young Mexican girls to help them pass away the nights. One of the men remembered her fondly. "I could stand at full attention, my head flung back," he said, "and she would just stand there in front of me flat-footed and drop one of those cherry-tipped melons of hers into my mouth. To a man on the eve of death, it was the taste of paradise." She was a businesswoman who knew how to make a business flourish.

But there was a war to be fought. The Mexicans under General Santa Ana decided to attack Saltillo. Taylor chose to take his army and meet them out in a neighboring area called Buena Vista.

Sarah, never one to sit behind the sidelines, chose to be in the thick of it during the battle. The men would need some soiled angels of mercy. She closed down the American House and loaded up her wagons with her girls and all the supplies she could carry. She set herself up next to the doctor's tent. The time would be coming soon when he would need all the help he could get. She would help with the wounded. She would carry them out of the battlefields. She would dress their wounds.

When everything was set up, in anticipation of the battle, Sarah climbed up the 6,000-foot hill, the highest point in the

Sarah Bowman, "The Great Western," a painting by Samuel Chamberlain, photo by Herb Orth, *Life Magazine* (©1956, Time Warner, Inc.)

area. There she watched 20,000 Mexican soldiers spread out across the Buena Vista plain. The view was spectacular. She watched as the Mexican bands played music for a solemn Mass as the priests and clergy processed into the field to give benediction and communion. It was an awesome sight, made even more so by the knowledge that General Taylor had a mere 5,000 men in his opposing force, many of them new untried recruits.

She watched as the battle began. Later, during the fighting, Sarah and Dutch Mary strung kettles of hot coffee across their shoulders and walked onto the battlefield. Sarah always carried two pistols in her belt. She was an excellent shot. If she had to, she was ready to fight.

One time a young soldier, panicked by the horrifying din of battle, yelled at her that all was lost. "Retreat," he said, "we're all going to be killed."

Such panic was not to be tolerated in the heat of war. Sarah turned around and punched him in the face, sending him sprawling. Then, in case he hadn't yet figured out her message, she roared obscenities at him. "No bunch of Mexicans are going to whip old Taylor. Now get out there and fight. I'm right behind you."

The men cheered. She gave them courage to go on. With their Bowie knives between their teeth, they literally hacked the enemy to pieces. The Mexican soldiers began to scream, "Devils, red devils!" Then they began to retreat.

Voluptuous in the boudoir and tough in the battlefield, there was a soft side to this woman. She wept when she heard that Captain George Lincoln, a cousin to Abraham Lincoln, had been killed. Sarah had known Captain Lincoln from the time when her first husband had signed up with the military. They had been friends that long while. Often he had come to dine at her American House. She went alone into the quiet battlefield that night and searched among the dead until she found his body. No one was going to desecrate his remains. Tenderly she brought him back for a decent burial. Later she bought the Captain's horse at a considerable expense. In time, she sent the horse back to Lincoln's mother. It was a gesture that no one forgot.

The men noticed. They remembered their great golden girl,

Sarah. She bound their wounds, nurtured their bodies and when they were well again, she and her girls gave those same bodies joyful, exuberant pleasure.

The signing of the treaty of Guadalupe-Hidalgo ended the war. General Winfield Scott awarded Sarah a commission of a brevet colonel for her bravery and services to the army. She was also given a pension by the United States government.

After the war, a small unit made up of First and Second Dragoons and a battery of light artillery, headed by Lieutenant Colonel John Washington, decided to continue westward to occupy the areas of New Mexico and California.

Sarah went to Colonel Washington riding a great white horse, wearing a brilliant royal purple riding habit and sporting a cavalier's hat decorated with a white plume. "Colonel Washington, I'd like permission to join the unit and travel west with you."

"Sarah," Colonel Washington replied, "you must be married to one of our military men and then be mustered in as a laundress before I can allow you to join us."

Sarah gave the Colonel a snappy salute and said, "All right, Major, I'll marry the whole squadron and you thrown in, but I intend to go along."

Riding down the line of assembled soldiers, Sarah called out, "Who wants a wife with $15,000 and the biggest legs in the country?" The men stared at her dumbfounded. This was an offer that took their breath away. "Come on, gentlemen," she laughed with a toss of her head, "don't all speak at once. Who is to be the lucky man?"

Finally a man in Company E, named Davis, spoke up. "I've no objection to making you my wife, if there is a clergyman here to tie the knot."

Our heroine chuckled and replied, "Bring your blanket to my tent tonight and I reckon that I can teach you to tie some knots that will be satisfying to you."

While the unit was traveling in Mexico near the ciy of Chihuahua, Sarah had a change of heart about Davis. Surrounded by men considerably smaller than herself, Sarah one day saw a man among a group of New Mexican traders whose size and strength were compatible with her own. Her first view of him was while he was bathing. Completely taken with his impressive proportions, she contrived every way she could to get a chance to meet him. When finally she did, she blushingly told him of her desire for a man of her own dimension. "We'll fit together right," she said.

Impressed by her curvacious charms, he succumbed to her request. Davis was almost forgotten. She told him it was over. She had found a Herculean new love.

Sarah did not continue to California with the army, nor did she remain with her great Adonis. She became ill and upon recovery set up a small hotel on the southern side of the Rio Grande River at El Paso del Norte, a town now known as Ciudad Juarez. There she catered to the needs of settlers en route to the West. It soon proved impossible to meet the needs of the hordes of settlers anxiously trying to keep provisioned while traveling to the California gold fields. Food and livestock were often stolen. This was the first time in years that Sarah was separated from the protection of the army. Times were hard. She missed her soldiers.

Sarah decided to move across the river to the American side and there, with a partner, started a hotel and restaurant. Things went well for awhile. Her dining room attracted many patrons because of her good cooking and her courteous and amiable ways. But in the end, she was obliged to close down the hotel and turn it over to the army as its headquarters.

It was time for Sarah to move on. Then she met Albert Bowman of the Second Dragoons. Although she was fifteen years older than he, she never told him that, acknowledging only to a nine-year difference. They soon married.

She had been a camp follower for years. She loved to wear vivid colors, violet and red velvet, and glamorous hats. She always carried a pistol. But, she was at the same time modest and womanly, kind and motherly. Bowman had been born in Germany, had migrated to New York City, was an upholsterer for awhile and then joined the army, becoming a sergeant. In spite of their diverse backgrounds, the attraction was a strong one. They continued the relationship for almost sixteen years.

On November 30, 1852, Sergeant Bowman was discharged from the army and the couple moved to Fort Yuma on the Colorado River. Sarah Bowman became the first white woman to live there. She helped provide an army hospital. She started a hotel and tavern where the men could go drink, dance and gamble. Except for a brief sojourn away during the Civil War, she was to remain in Fort Yuma for the rest of her life.

At that time Fort Yuma was under the command of a Major Samuel Peter Heintzelman. Not happy with his posting, this small, bearded, somewhat fuss-budget of a man revealed in his journals a love-hate attraction toward Sarah. He could not reconcile himself with the fact that although Sarah was married, a good cook, generous and kindly, she provided the men with young Mexican and Indian girls who stayed with her but lived with specific men at night.

He was to eventually hire her to fix his meals and to clean his house. The relationship was one of constant negotiation, relieved by a mutual love of gossip. When the Major realized that he was going to be reassigned, he began to think of selling his considerable possessions to have sufficient cash for his next billeting. Sarah wanted to buy. After all, life at the fort had few luxuries. At times the weather was so hot it felt as if it could fry a lizard's tongue.

The hard-headed but charming businesswoman and the cagey military man constantly manipulated each other to see

Early drawing of Ft. Yuma
(Courtesy Arizona Historical Society, Tucson)

who could achieve the upper financial hand in these negotiations.

Sarah also played a small but significant part in the story of Olive Oatman, whose family had been horridly massacred not far from the fort. Sarah was a participant in the group that helped to bury the tragic remains of the family. Years later, when Olive was finally released from captivity by the Indians, Sarah provided housing for Olive upon her return to the fort.

Sarah also took on the task of adopting Mexican orphan children and taught them the skills of cooking and tavern keeping, helping them to become self-sufficient.

Her death was by no stray bullet or marauding Indian arrow. Instead she succumbed to the bite of a poisonous insect and died

Gravestone of Sarah Bowman at National Cemetery, Presidio, San Francisco (Courtesy Arizona Historical Society Library, Tucson)

when she was fifty-four years old.

Her funeral included the complete Catholic rites, and full military honors. Everyone in town processed solemnly to the music of a military band and a three-gun salute was fired over her flag-draped casket. Many felt the sting of tears as they remembered this splendid woman. Years later, after her remains had been disinterred to the Presidio National Cemetery in San Francisco, the city of Yuma was to honor her by giving Sarah Bowman the title of "First Citizen of Yuma."

Circumstance: being over a foot taller than the majority of the women of her time, having striking good looks, courage and devotion destined Sarah Bowman to live an extraordinary life. She will always be remembered as "a woman to look up to."

BIBLIOGRAPHY

Chamberlain, Samuel E., *My Confession*, Harper & Brothers, New York, 1956.

Elliott, James F., "The Great Western, Sarah Bowman, Mother and Mistress to the U.S. Army," *The Journal of Arizona History*, Spring, 1989.

Heintzelman, Major Samuel P., Transcription of Journal, January 1, 1851-December 1853, "Concerning the establishment of an army post at the junction of the Colorado and the Gila Rivers," Creola Blackwell, Transcriber, Yuma County Historical Society, Yuma.

McGaw, William C., *Southwest Saga,* Golden West Publishers, Phoenix, Arizona, 1988.

Trimble, Marshall, "Yuma's First Citizen," *The Arizona Republic*, Feb. 24, 1985.

Western Writers of America, Hamilton, Nancy, *The Women Who Made the West*, Doubleday & Company, Inc., Garden City, New York, 1980.

Yavapai Gold

Arizona probably has more stories about gold mines that have been lost and then found than any other state. To sit around a fire at night and listen to a tale of one man's journey to riches against incredible odds, creates moments when the listener believes that all that is needed is a little effort, a reaching out of a hand, to seize the chance at gaining a fabulous treasure. Here are several short stories about people who came to Arizona to hunt for gold and what happened to them.

Our first story begins in the early 1860s on a Missouri farm. A farmer named Henry Youngblood was experiencing hard times. Bank speculation and a drop in crop prices were causing many of the farmers great difficulties in meeting their mortgages. Henry Youngblood was not making enough income to pay his mortgage and support his family.

One day, Youngblood read in the local newspaper that gold had been discovered out west in a place called Arizona. The article stated that some prospectors were making fortunes seemingly overnight. That evening he talked with his wife.

"You know, my dear," he said, "I'm a hard-working man and I know that if I could get myself out to this Arizona, I'd work and work and I know that I could find us a little gold. We don't need a lot of gold. We just need enough to get us through these hard times."

Henry Youngblood decided to go to a rich neighbor and borrow some money, just enough to cover his expenses. The neighbor wanted something as a guarantee to back up the loan. Henry Youngblood put up his farm as collateral. Then he took the stage to Prescott, Arizona.

When he arrived, the first thing that happened was that Youngblood became ill with some sort of flu or virus. He had to spend the next few weeks in a narrow bed in his small boardinghouse room. To make matters worse, he received a letter from his wife telling him that the rich neighbor, who had once been a rival of Youngblood's for his wife's hand, had come to her and told her that if she didn't pay him the money, he would take over the farm as his collateral right, and throw her and the children out of their home.

Desperately, Henry dragged himself out of bed, took what few possessions he had and sold them in order to buy some mining supplies. He started walking south, southeast toward the Bradshaw Mountains. When he finally arrived in this rugged area, he began to prospect for gold. Every day from early morning until sunset, he would take his pick and shovel and work on any terrain that he thought looked promising. He worked as hard as he could, but he found no gold. Every day he continued to pick and shovel and prospect, but still he found no gold.

Then he ran out of food, yet he continued to pick and shovel and prospect looking for gold. Still he found none. One afternoon, some days later, there was a cold wind blowing through those Bradshaw Mountains and Henry Youngblood was chilled, hungry and exhausted. He flung himself down in front of a huge boulder and lifted his face toward the heavens, crying out, "Is this to be my fate? Am I to die of starvation out in these God-forsaken mountains? Is my family to be thrown off the farm? Is this all there is?"

Suddenly, out of the corner of his eye, he saw a twinkling in the boulder above him. Oh, he thought to himself, it's more of that fool's gold. But some inner sense of hope prompted him to get up one more time and examine the boulder. There in the stone before him was a vein of quartz the width of a man's hand. In the shimmering light he could see tiny nuggets of pure gold.

Youngblood began to act like a madman. He started to tear and pick at the nuggets of gold. He noticed that the vein went right up the boulder and continued for a great distance among the rocks of the hill. Here within his grasp was a fortune of gold worth millions of dollars.

In a short while, Henry Youngblood had a nice pile of gold nuggets. Putting the gold in his pockets, he then examined the countryside surrounding him. He took careful calculations of exactly where he was located. He also carefully covered up all signs of his activities, camouflaging the boulder as best he could, and went back to Prescott.

When he arrived in town, he took the nuggets and sold them and purchased a complete mining outfit. He bought himself several mules, saddlebags and a goodly amount of food. Then he went right back to the Bradshaw Mountains and to his newly-found claim.

Within a month's time, he had mined enough gold to fill his saddlebags full. Moreover, he had traced the vein to its origin in the hills and he knew that he was the owner of one of the richest gold claims in all of Arizona.

Once again, he carefully covered up all signs of his activities. Then he placed the filled saddlebags onto the mules. Just as he was about to leave, a sharp pain stabbed him in the chest, his arm went limp, and one leg collapsed under him. The pain was excruciating, but he was able to drag himself with his last breaths of consciousness to one of the mules. He crawled onto the mule and smacked the animal in the direction of Prescott.

A surge of excitement swept through the townspeople of Prescott when they saw the mules come into the town loaded with gold with this half-dead man draped over one of them.

People crowded 'round. They brought him a doctor. They brought him something to drink. They found him a bed and some nursing care and all the time they kept asking, "Where, where, where did you find the gold?"

Henry whispered through his pain, "I can't tell you right now, I'm too sick. But when I get better, I will tell you because there is enough gold out there for all of us."

In time, Youngblood did get better and once again people crowded around him asking, "Where, where, where did you find the gold?"

"Look," he said, "I must get back to Missouri. My wife and children have been thrown off our farm and they need my help. But I intend to come back and then I'll tell you where I found the gold. I'm not exaggerating, there is enough for all of us."

Packing up his gold, he placed it on the stage and returned to Missouri. When Henry Youngblood arrived at the stagecoach station, his family greeted him with joy and excitement. His wife and children kissed and hugged him, laughing and crying all at once. "Look, my darlings," he said, hugging them and kissing them, "look at all the gold I've brought. We can buy a bigger farm and if there are more hard times it won't matter. We have enough gold here to get us through lots of hard times and there's more where this comes from."

The Youngblood family were continuing their happy, tearful reunion when suddenly another sharp pain stabbed Henry

Youngblood in the chest. His arm went limp. His leg collapsed under him and he fell to the ground. His wife cradled him in her arms.

He looked up at her as she held him and said, "My dear, if somehow I don't get better this time, let me tell you, let me explain where to find the gold." His face was contorted with pain as he spoke, "You go to a place called Prescott, Arizona. Then go 40 miles south, southeast until you reach the Bradshaw Mountains. There's a large boulder there and, and, . . ." and he died in his wife's arms.

There are two theories about Henry Youngblood's vein of gold. One group of people say that about a year-and-a-half later his vein was rediscovered and became the basis of one of the greatest gold mines in all of Arizona, the Vulture Mine. Others disagree, saying that the Vulture is located just south of Wickenburg and Henry Youngblood stated that the gold was to be found in the Bradshaw Mountains. These people believe that someday, someone will be out walking in those Bradshaw Mountains after a heavy rain and there, beneath their feet, will be Henry Youngblood's vein of gold.

Author's note: In a recent discussion with the owner of an Alaskan gold mine, I discovered that there is a club of gold mine owners in Arizona. This person says that there are about 18 small family or individually-held mines which do some producing in the Bradshaws.

Vulture Gold

What inner energy, what thought process is involved in making a man decide to search for gold? At first perhaps there is desire for adventure, or a gambler's sense of hope that he has latched onto a path to luck. But what keeps a man making the conscious deliberation year after year to go on in the face of knowledge that the odds are stacked against a win, that failure is the bottom line of the game?

In 1819, Heinrich Wickenburg was born in the small German town of Essen. In 1847, when he was 28 years old, Heinrich, like so many other Germans, left his homeland to come to the United States for the purpose of finding a financial opportunity that would make him rich. He landed in New York City with little money. But he did not remain in the East like so many of the German immigrants, who found small farms to run or took on a factory job or worked in a slaughter house living out their lives in borderline poverty, growing old before their time from relentless hard work and long hours. Henry, as he chose to call himself, was able to get hired as a fireman on the Cortez, a steamship going to California by way of Cape Horn.

Lured by the great gold discoveries of 1848 and 1849, Henry Wickenburg spent 13 years searching for a rich claim without success. It was always someone else who made the discovery, who found the bonanza.

Then in 1861, California experienced a severe winter. The weather was the worst that anyone could remember. Rivers such as the Sacramento flooded, destroying crops and grazing land; cattle were left stranded without enough to eat. Many died. Henry, always looking for a way to make money, took to skinning the dead cattle for their hides as hides were fetching extremely high prices. Everything went smoothly for awhile as his new business venture began to bring him a comfortable income. Henry, for the first time since he had arrived in the United States, was making financial gains.

But the ranchers and farmers were frustrated over the loss of their cattle investment and any hope of a profit. Realizing that Wickenburg was making money from their adversity, they sought legal advice. Did this not constitute an illegal trespass? But the law progressed slowly and the ranchers and farmers grew angry. Their mutterings began to coalesce and focus on Henry, that damned German. Soon the talk exploded into demands for action.

When Henry heard the rumors that the cattlemen were talking about taking the law into their own hands by punishing him as an example to others who might wish to undertake similar activities, he decided it was time to start anew somewhere else.

Arizona was being touted as the next place to find bonanza gold, since the California rush was no longer yielding new discoveries. Coming across California, Henry crossed the Colorado River and joined a small prospecting group which included two other men, Buckskin Smith and a man named Morris. The three of them traveled along the Bill Williams River making camp not far from the present town of Congress.

While in this vicinity, Indians pointed out a small mountain which later became known as Rich Hill, saying that there was strange-colored rock to be seen there. The prospectors never followed through on the Indians' suggestion because they were low on supplies and the possibility of attack by unfriendly Indians was a constant concern. A decision to break camp was made, leaving no time to explore. Wickenburg, impressed with the Indians' story, made careful observations of the exact location of the hill. It was his hope to find a way to return there at some later date to search for mineral wealth.

In the meantime, a California entrepreneur named Abraham H. Peeples undertook the organization of an expedition to search for gold in that same Indian-infested region of the territory of Arizona. Peeples hired Pauline Weaver, a part-native American, mountain man and trailblazer to guide his party.

Weaver's Cherokee mother gave him the name of Quah-a-ha-na which means "good talker," but his father called him Paulino which he eventually shortened to Pauline. Born in Tennessee in 1800, Weaver grew to be a tall, well-muscled man. He came to Arizona around 1830 seeking his fortune as a trapper of beaver pelts. When hunting and trapping no longer offered the financial returns that he originally had hoped for, Weaver took up prospecting and guiding.

Members of the party met and crossed the Colorado River

into Arizona at a point just north of present-day Ehrenberg. Weaver guided the group northeast, following traces of washes, into some low mountain areas. The expedition traveled toward the area in which Henry Wickenburg and his party had camped during the previous year.

Henry Wickenburg had planned to join the Peeples party, but by the time he reached the Arizona side of the Colorado River the expedition had already left. Disappointed at arriving too late, but resolved not to be left out of an opportunity to be in on any new gold discoveries, the thin but toughened six-footer decided to race after them. In spite of advice to wait and join with others because the Indians preferred to attack single victims, Henry, traveling cautiously, ever mindful not to allow himself to be observed at a distance, covered the two hundred miles alone through dangerous Apache territory. Eventually he did catch up with the party, but it was weeks too late.

One morning during the Peeple's expedition, Pauline Weaver noticed that several of the horses in the camp were missing. He sent a couple of the Mexican wranglers to search for the horses which were soon found. Not only were the wandering horses brought back, but the wranglers brought back some interesting-looking rock they had found on a nearby hill. Weaver was curious about the color of the rock and he led his prospecting group to the hill. Using his hunting knife, he pried out a few specimens from the ground and carried them to Yuma to be appraised. The samples were analyzed and identified as gold. Mayhem broke out as the prospectors staked out claims. The news spread like wildfire as men appeared from everywhere to search the surrounding countryside.

The hill, now referred to as Rich Hill, had nuggets of gold which were found simply lying about. More gold was located at nearby Antelope Hill. These two hills were to become the richest single placer discovery ever found in Arizona. Placer gold is caused when glacier activity and erosion wear away the surrounding rock leaving the valuable mineral ore exposed.

To have come this close to finding a fortune in gold only to see it slip from one's grasp would have discouraged most men, but not Henry Wickenburg. Even after close to 15 years of relentless disappointment, he was determined that his turn must come one day. Wickenburg took to the trails to prospect. Henry had

Henry Wickenburg
(Courtesy Arizona Historical Society Library, Tucson)

heard of two men who had recently been found in the desert having been murdered by the Indians. Lying next to their bodies was a large amount of very valuable gold ore. The Indians, not yet aware of the value of gold ore, were more interested in stealing guns, food, clothing and animals. To Henry, this indicated that there might be other outcroppings of gold in this general vicinity.

For a while he traveled with two other prospectors, a man named Von Webber and another man named Green who became ill. Exhausted from the rough mountainous desert terrain, Von Webber and Green wanted to abandon the search and set up camp to rest and recover their strength. Wickenburg continued on alone, somewhat discouraged but unwilling to give up. He traveled south into the desert to an area west of the Hassayampa River where he found himself attracted to the appearance of the country, particularly to a shelf of white quartz outcroppings.

Once again traveling alone through dangerous countryside, and anxious not to overlook a possible opportunity, Henry was to have another problem confront him. He noticed that his mule was no longer able or willing to keep up the pace. Stranded in the desert miles from nowhere, Wickenburg tried to force the animal, only to have the mule stop and refuse to move altogether. Sitting down in the dirt a short distance from the burro to try to think of a solution to this new difficulty, Henry Wickenburg noticed a vulture slowly circling overhead. The vulture soared down from the sky, and landed near the stalled mule, eyeing it proprietarily.

All the years of frustration welled up inside of Henry. An all-consuming rage emanated from deep within his being, and the usually gentle Wickenburg picked up a rock lying nearby and threw it at the bird. The vulture fluttered away in fright, but the rock seemed to fall apart as it hit the ground.

Henry tried to settle himself back from his anger, to move back from this edge of madness. As calm returned to him in that quiet desert setting, he remembered the disintegrating rock. Curious as to why the rock appeared to fall apart, Wickenburg went over to examine the scattered pieces and discovered a large nugget of gold. Scarcely able to breathe, he tried to settle his thoughts. Had his chance finally materialized or was this a fluke? It couldn't be, he thought to himself; he had to have come upon a gold discovery, but of what size and worth?

Exploring the surrounding area, Henry Wickenburg located a rich lode, a vein of gold that was nearly fifteen feet wide. Racing back to his prospecting companions, Von Webber and Green, he excitedly told them of his discovery, only to have the prospectors dismiss his descriptions as the ramblings of a man who had stayed too long in the desert sun. While Henry returned to the site of his discovery, the two men left for Tucson, ostensibly to get more supplies. They never returned.

Right then Henry staked out as much of the area as the Arizona law would allow, placing posts on the corners of three 300-square foot claims. Filing by himself, he called his find the Vulture Mine and it proved itself to be not the daydreams of a worn-out prospector, but a fabulously rich producer of gold. When Von Webber eventually learned of the great strike made by Wickenburg, he went to court to claim a financial interest in the mine. Wickenburg refused to acknowledge any right of Von Webber and the courts, after a long legal battle, found in Wickenburg's favor.

Vulture Mine
(Courtesy Sharlot Hall Museum Archives, Prescott)

Luck had finally smiled upon this determined German, but problems still hampered his efforts. Water is needed to process gold and the nearest water was to be found in the Hassayampa River some 12 miles away. In those early months, many of the men who were transporting gold ore for washing at the river were killed by Apaches.

Another miner named Charles Genung came to Henry's camp. A system of processing the ore was needed that would work in these waterless conditions. A mill needed to be built. Wickenburg did not have the necessary funds or the knowledge to know what to do. He had gold without the wherewithal to mine and refine it. Genung, an experienced mining man, showed Wickenburg how to build and use a circular in-ground *arrastra* for grinding gold. By using animal power such as mules, burros, horses or oxen, to pull a heavy stone over the ore to break up and release the gold, less water was required in the processing.

At that point Henry decided to sell rights to the ore for $15 a ton. This gave him the necessary cash to build and outfit as many as 40 *arrastras* for grinding the gold and to hopefully save for building a mill. Having a large number of men coming to work the claim helped make everyone reasonably safe from Apache raids by virtue of their numbers.

Water continued to be a problem. At one point Henry was transporting water from the Hassayampa on mule and selling it for ten cents a gallon. In time the surface gold was all mined out and Wickenburg did not have the mining skill or financial resources to search for underground gold and mine it.

Having no training in mineralogy, Henry had no way of realizing the extent of his claim. Wickenburg eventually sold the mine to a Mr. Phelps, a rich man from New York, for $85,000. Phelps then funded underground exploration and the building of a processing mill.

Although Henry had finally found his bonanza mine, his sense of business timing and his lack of mining knowledge worked against him. He was to have no financial part in the income of over $2.5 million in gold that the Vulture Mining Company produced during the years of 1866 to 1872. The mine had in fact more gold ore than that, but a goodly amount was high-graded or stolen by the miners during those early months of production. When the rich ore was fairly mined out, the mining then continued on a low-grade ore which had initially been passed over. Various estimates of the entire financial gain made at the Vulture Mine range from $7 to $12 million. Translated into contemporary financial terms, that return would have been worth over a billion dollars.

Wickenburg used some of the money acquired in the sale of the Vulture to buy himself a farm near the mine where he was to live for the rest of his life. He also tried to invest his money in such schemes as Jack Swilling's irrigation project for the Salt River Valley. Most of his investments proved unprofitable. Over the years, the size of his capital continued to diminish. Henry remained on his farm where he also ran a general store. In 1873, he was elected to serve as a member of the House of

Representatives for the territorial legislature.

He died at the age of 86 in 1905. The official cause of death was declared suicide, although many felt that Henry gave no indication of a desire to do away with his life. No suicide note was found. People who knew him recalled no indications of depression. These people believe he was murdered. They believed that someone came to the store and overpowered the old man in order to rob him. No evidence was ever found to substantiate a verdict of murder.

A mining town named after Henry Wickenburg developed in the area near the Hassayampa River. Some 53 miles from Phoenix, the town, which had come close to becoming a ghost town after the Vulture Mine stopped producing gold, continues to flourish to this day, resurrected in part by the discovery of gold mines in the Bradshaw Mountains. The town lives with the same kind of conscious deliberation and determination that prompted its namesake to go on when others had long since given up.

What causes a man to search for gold, and to go on year after gruelling year looking for treasure when the odds are stacked against a win and the bottom-line is often failure?

BIBLIOGRAPHY

Allen, J. S., "Henry Wickenburg and the Vulture Mine," *Federal Writers' Project*, Prescott, Arizona, State Capital Library.

Arizona Gazette, "Henry Wickenburg," May 15, 1905, page 1, column 3.

The Arizona Republic, "Death of a Pioneer," May 15, 1905.

Farish, Thomas, *History of Arizona*, Arizona State Historian, Volume II, page 211.

Goff, John S., *Arizona Biographical Dictionary*, Black Mountain Press, Cave Creek, Arizona, 1983.

McClintock, James H., *Arizona, the Youngest State*, Volume II, The S. J. Clarke Publishing Company, Chicago, 1916, pages 404-405.

Miller, Joseph, Editor, *Arizona Cavalcade, the Turbulent Times*, Hastings House, Publishers, New York, 1952.

Pare, Madeline Ferrin, in collaboration with Bert M. Fireman, *Arizona Pageant, A Short History of the 48th State*, Arizona Historical Foundation, Tempe, Arizona, 1967.

Saturday Review, "Wickenburg History," June 18, 1904, page 1, column 1, Phoenix, Arizona.

Wagoner, Jay J., *Arizona's Heritage*, Peregrine Smith, Inc. Santa Barbara and Salt Lake City, 1977.

Williams, Governor Jack, *From the Ground Up, Stories of Arizona's Mines and Early Mineral Discoveries*, Phelps-Dodge Corporation, 1981.

Cyrus Gribble and the Vulture Mine

Gold makes some men rich. Gold makes some men fools.

Cyrus Gribble, the superintendent of the Vulture Mine, thought that he was smarter and more clever than any other man. In fact, Cyrus Gribble was absolutely certain that there was not a bandit alive who could possibly outsmart him, particularly that supposedly clever but dastardly bandit named Francisco Vega.

Francisco Vega had acquired his reputation after a series of murders and robberies of some miners who were working Henry Wickenburg's gold concentrate in the early days of the Vulture. If the Indians didn't get the miners, it was Francisco Vega and his gang who did. Also, this deadly bandit was held responsible for the murders of the Barney Martin family. This pioneer family had sold their holdings in the Hassayampa area and were en route with the cash from the sale to settle in Phoenix. The family was last seen when they stopped at Seymore where Harry Cowell was keeping a station way-house. The Martins were expected in Phoenix and when they did not show up, a search party eventually found their burned remains near Castle Creek Mountain. The large amount of money which they had been carrying was gone.

Now, in those days, around the year of 1888, there were no railroads in Arizona. The only way to transport gold bullion from the Vulture Mine to a bank was to haul it the 60 miles to Phoenix. Phoenix was the closest place with a bank that had a large, solid safe.

For some years, the superintendent of the mine, a man named Elmore, feared this bandit, Francisco Vega, and was certain that Vega wanted nothing more than to rob the gold taken from the mine. To assure that the notorious robber would not be successful in holding up the Vulture's gold, Elmore had devised a complicated scheme to get the processed ore to Phoenix.

First, he told only a very few trusted people exactly when the gold was going to be sent from the mine. Then he would send several types of teams, each at varied times and on slightly different routes. No one except Elmore knew if the gold was traveling on a slow-moving freight wagon, several fast teams of horses, or with a couple of single riders on horseback. Sometimes the gold was with none of these, having yet to leave the mine. Elmore would never accurately divulge when the gold had arrived safely in Phoenix until a much later date. Consequently, no one ever knew for certain who had the gold until it had long been deposited in the Phoenix bank. This method of Superintendent Elmore's was very successful and for years Francisco Vega had never been able to steal any of the Vulture's gold.

But then Cyrus Gribble became superintendent of the Vulture Mine. Gribble made fun of Elmore's fear of the notorious bandit. He told anyone who would listen that he had his own method for transporting the gold. Sneaking around, having six different ways of getting the gold to Phoenix was not for him. From now on, he would announce to everyone exactly when the gold was going to be shipped. He had a plan. He would ship the gold to Phoenix in a way that would absolutely guarantee its safety.

On the morning after a bullion clean-up, Cyrus Gribble would take the gold the 60 miles to Phoenix in broad daylight, using a pair of fast-footed black mares. These horses were the fastest anyone had seen in a long while. He would take along as the driver, Johnny Johnson, one of the best. Gribble would personally sit next to the driver holding a sawed-off, double-barreled shotgun loaded with the heaviest buckshot. In addition to that, he also employed an outrider, Charles Doolittle, who was heavily-armed and was a crack shot, to ride about 100 yards ahead of the buggy to scout for trouble. Cyrus Gribble liked to brag that he could get the gold to Phoenix in spite of the robber Vega, in spite of the Devil and in spite of anyone else who would dare to try to rob the Vulture gold.

Months went by and Cyrus Gribble continued to use his method of transporting the gold to Phoenix. Many folks tried to tell him that he was foolish to persist with this plan, but Cyrus Gribble merely laughed at them. "Haven't months gone by without so much as the least little incident? Isn't that proof enough that my plan is an absolute success?" People just shook their heads in disagreement.

Then one day, March 19, 1888, everything changed. The day

The Vulture Mine in early 1900s
(Courtesy Arizona Historical Society, Tucson)

for transporting $3,000 of bullion started off just like any other day. The ride was uneventful until the outrider and the buggy had traveled about 20 miles of the 60-mile journey. At that point there was a deep but wide arroyo made from some desert flash flooding. Within the arroyo, growing in a depression, was a clump of greasewood shrubs. Someone had added more greasewood branches to the original clump to make a thick screen for two men to hide behind.

The outrider passed safely by the two hidden bandits, without noticing them. As he took his horse out of the arroyo and onto the desert, he was quickly shot by a man lying hidden in a dug-out rifle pit. By the time Gribble and Johnson heard the shot and realized what was happening, they had already passed the greasewood shrubs. With their backs to the bandits, they neither saw the robbers get up to shoot them nor were they in a position to easily return fire. Fatally wounded, Gribble tried to raise his shotgun to shoot and only succeeded in killing one of the black mares pulling the buggy.

The first person to come along after the robbery and murders wasted no time. Riding at a gallop all the way to the sheriff's office in Phoenix, he gave the alarm. A posse was immediately organized which included such notables as the district attorney, Frank Cox, Jim Murphy, Frank Prothero, Tom Davenport, Jack Halbert and Bud Gray.

In spite of being many hours behind the assassins, the posse, with a speed only the most daredevil of horsemen could handle, traveled from Phoenix to the scene of the murders and then took up trailing the robbers. As far as could be ascertained there had been five in the gang. After grabbing the heavy brick of gold bullion, the bandits rode west toward the Hassayampa River. At the river the gang split up in order to confuse their pursuers. Two turned north following the river bed. The other three crossed the river and continued in a westerly direction attempting perhaps to make it to the Colorado River.

During the third night on the trail, the posse believed that they had caught up with the bandits and had surrounded them. Concerned that they did not have enough men to successfully take on a shoot-out, they sent one of the posse, Tom Davenport, back to the Vulture Mine for reinforcements.

By the time extra help had arrived, the fugitives had buried the heavy load and had managed to escape by slipping out of the area. They had been unable to divide the bar of gold because it had been alloyed with a metal which could not be broken with an axe.

Once again the posse set out on the trail, at times getting so close to the fleeing robbers that shots were exchanged. It now became every man for himself, and the robbers, each going his individual way, were able to give the posse the slip. One of them, a man by the name of Inocente Martinez, was able to return to his home in Phoenix by a roundabout trail. A young Mexican boy who accompanied him managed to disappear. The other, a Francisco Valenzuela, managed to get across the border to Mexico where he escaped extradition back to the United States. Frustrated with the lack of success, the posse returned to Phoenix.

Although there was no concrete proof of Inocente's involvement in the robbery, his home was watched. Eventually he returned to the place where the posse had originally surrounded three members of the gang. There he was caught as he tried to dig up the massive gold bar. Inocente decided to fight it out with the posse and was killed in the ensuing battle. The gold was then returned to the owners of the Vulture Mine.

But the famous Francisco Vega, the notorious leader of the gang, and his companion had simply disappeared. Six months later, in the town of Fairbank, some 10 miles from Tombstone, not far from the Mexican border, the sheriff arrested two men. One of the men was a short, handsome Mexican with black hair and white skin. The other was a tall black man. The tall black man was observed to be wearing the gold Elgin watch that Johnny Johnson had worn on the day of the murders and the Vulture robbery. Both men were indicted for murder by the grand jury of Maricopa County.

The court trial was a furiously-fought legal battle. The prosecution produced witnesses who swore that the two men were seen around the Vulture camp a day or two prior to the murders. Another witness gave evidence that he had loaned the Elgin to Johnson that day to allow him to clock the speed of the two mares. He claimed he knew it was his Elgin because he had broken the watch when he had been thrown from a bucking horse in Texas and had had it repaired there. He pointed to marks on the watch to back up his identification.

The defense brought in a ranch owner from Florence who swore that at the time of the robbery the two men were on the ranch in his employ. The prosecution's case was destroyed when the defendants were able to produce two Phoenix jewelers who swore that the watch could not have sustained that kind of damage. In order to repair such damage a special tool would have had to be used and no such tool was available outside the factory of manufacture and a few major cities in the United States. The jury acquitted both men who were then set free. Neither man ever admitted to being the notorious Francisco Vega.

As for Cyrus Gribble's method of transporting gold to Phoenix, no one was ever so foolish as to use it again.

BIBLIOGRAPHY

Arizona Weekly Citizen, March 24, 1888, page 2, column 4, an account of the murder.
Phoenix Daily Herald, July 2, 1888, page 2, column 4, reward for apprehending the murderer.
Goodman, Burt, "Bandits on the Hassayampa," *Scottsdale Progress*, December 16, 1988, page 3.
Miller, Joseph, Editor, *Arizona Cavalcade, the Turbulent Times*, Hastings House, Publishers, New York, 1962, pages 78-87.

A Man Named Poston

In traveling around the state of Arizona, have you often observed the word "Poston" on buildings and streets? Do you know about the town called Poston? If you are shaking your head in puzzlement over your lack of familiarity with the name, you are not alone. Yet, history and the very existence of Arizona owe a debt of gratitude to a man named Poston.

After the 1500s, when the Spanish explorers had abandoned their expeditions in search of the seven cities of Cibola, the fabled cities of gold and treasure, Arizona became a forgotten place. Periodically a flag, Spanish, Mexican or New Mexican, would be posted on its soil to reflect the current political situation. Before the United States acquired Arizona, no more than a dozen American mountain men and miners attempted to penetrate one of the few places in the continent of North America that could boast of seven life-zone levels. Until this country claimed the vast reaches of Arizona desert, mountain and canyon, the land had been left unexplored, unconsidered and unwanted.

On December 31, 1853, just one day after the signing of the Gadsden treaty, which purchased the southern section of Arizona from Mexico, an exploring party sailed from San Francisco. This group was headed by a man, a dreamer of utopias, who was destined to carve a territory and a state out of this uncompromising wilderness, give it a name and force it to be recognized by an unwilling and uninterested Congress.

His name was Charles Debrille Poston. Born in Hardin County, Kentucky, on April 20, 1825, orphaned when he was just 12 years old, Charles Poston studied the law, married, fathered a child and settled down to the life of a practicing attorney much like his contemporary, Abraham Lincoln. But he was a dreamer and a romantic with no outlet for his visions until the gold discoveries in California inflamed the imaginations of thousands of people. Like so many others, Charles Poston became hopelessly afflicted with the yellow mineral fever.

Leaving his wife and daughter in the hands of relatives, he set off for California, hoping to carve out a prosperous life for his family and himself. Thus began an odyssey that would bring him equal portions of fame, wealth, recognition, loneliness and poverty.

Taking on the position of chief clerk in the San Francisco custom house, Charles Poston soon found himself in the employ of an agent for the family of General Augustino de Iturbide, who had inherited a large grant of land in what they believed was the new territory and wanted it located and explored for its resources.

Poston helped organize an expedition of 30 men, including several mining engineers, among whom was Christian Herman Ehrenberg. The party sailed to Sonora, Mexico. The journey did not live up to the high expectations of the leaders of the group. Their ship was blown off course. When they finally were able to get back on route, moving toward their destination, their hopes for a successful sea journey were further complicated. Caught in unexpected heavy seas, the ship was dashed against the rocks. The men were barely able to reach land safely before the ship sank. Once in Mexico, conditions did not improve. They were greeted with hostility by the Mexicans, still angry over losing so much of their land in the war with the United States. Eventually, after some days of tense negotiation, Poston and the rest of the party were given free access to travel to the new territory.

Their explorations revealed the many possibilities of this land. Old Mexican silver mines were found. Specimens of gold, silver and copper were collected. Decaying missionary churches were located. Although everyone searched diligently for the boundaries to the Iturbide land grant, they were never found and subsequently could not be established. But, by the end of the trip, Poston and Ehrenberg were convinced that this new land had enormous potential.

Still in his twenties, Poston already showed his ability to visualize the creation of new settlements, as well as his skill in cultivating friendships that would help him in the promotion of this territory.

Poston liked to tell a story about that initial journey. It happened when the group had reached the Colorado River and were ready to return to California. The only way to cross the river was by a ferryboat owned and operated by a Louis J. F. Jaeger. Because of hostile Indians in the area, there were risks involved in maintaining a ferry service. Therefore, Jaeger

Charles D. Poston, the "Father of Arizona"
(Courtesy Arizona Historical Society, Tucson.
National Archives photo no. 111-B-3183)

charged exceedingly high prices for passage. Poston had neither the desire nor the funds to pay the requested price to get his party across the Colorado. Jaeger refused to lower the price. It was a stand-off with seemingly no solution.

Here is where Poston's imaginative vision and resourcefulness came into play. Looking around him, he realized that one day a town or city would spring up on the banks of the Colorado River. Why not hurry the process along with a little promotion, he reasoned. Turning to the rest of his party, he suggested. "Let's sell city lots to passing travelers and make our money for the ferry that way." "Sell city lots," retorted members of his party, tired, hungry and exceedingly disgruntled. "There's nothing here but desert as far as the eye can see."

"True," countered Poston with a convivial smile, "but eventually a city will grow up near the river and Fort Yuma." With that rare ability to explain his vision of the future, Poston soon inspired the men with enthusiasm for his plan. Under the skilled surveying directions of Ehrenberg, the men, using sticks and stones and bits of string, began plotting out a city with a town square, roads and pier areas along the river.

Jaeger, intrigued by this buzz of activity, came over to find out what they were doing. With a show of salesman-like reluctance the men at first hesitated to tell him of their scheme. When Poston finally shared their plan with Jaeger, the ferryman was also caught up in that dream of the future and immediately bought sufficient parcels of land to allow the party funds for crossing the Colorado. In addition, many sites were sold in California, netting members of the expedition a tidy sum.

In San Diego, Poston and his party recorded their townsite, which was called Colorado City. Some believe that this was the beginning of Yuma. Others state that Yuma was located further south and that Colorado City never expanded to more than a temporary tent town.

Upon returning to San Francisco, Poston received a letter from Kentucky informing him that his wife was seriously ill and not expected to live. Poston quickly returned home. After a long convalescence, his wife recovered. Poston felt that now he could leave his family and travel to Washington, D.C. to see if it was possible to interest Congress in appropriating funds for further exploration of the territory. While in Washington, he renewed the acquaintance of Major Heintzelman, whom he had first met when the Major was in charge of Fort Yuma. Heintzelman shared Poston's enthusiasm for the potential of the area, not only for the opportunities to acquire wealth, but for the chance to create new frontier settlements. Both men realized that the United States was fast becoming a country where the frontier was disappearing.

Together, the two men were able to persuade the Texas Pacific Railroad to hire them to explore the land for a railroad route and to develop its mineral resources. The generosity of this first business client allowed the men to form the Sonora Exploring and Mining Company, with Heintzelman as its president and Poston as its managing director. Ehrenberg became a director in the new company, as well as its chief engineer and surveyor.

Money poured into this fledgling company and soon the directors could boast of two million in capital and $100,000 in cash for outfitting the expedition. Poston proceeded to San Antonio, which was considered at that time the best outfitting place in the Southwest. A man given to the grand gesture, encouraged by what seemed to be unlimited funds, he supplied the expedition royally. Mules, horses and wagons were loaded with provisions of every sort. There were tools, machinery, food, wines, clothing, books and many other luxuries, so that the travelers on the rugged trails would be assured of every possible comfort. All kinds of men flocked to join the expedition.

It took four months to travel the 762 miles to Arizona. Initially the journey was a delight. The first military fort they came to was run by a commander who was a *bon vivant* and had imported two French chefs to accommodate his culinary needs. Pleased at having the company of a raconteur such as Poston, he entertained his visitors lavishly. But such conditions did not last. A skirmish with the Apaches and constant rain made the trip difficult.

Arriving in Tucson in August of 1856, Poston, ever sensitive to the human condition and the general exhaustion of his party, gave the men a two-week holiday to rest and participate in the festival of St. Augustine which was in progress. After four months of traveling while remaining constantly alert to the possibility of an Indian attack, traversing swollen arroyos,

Tubac in 1863 with the Santa Rita Mountains in background
(Courtesy Arizona Historical Society Library, Tucson)

trekking through mud and trailless areas, Poston knew that the men needed the fiesta to help them overcome the stress and strain of the trip.

While his men were thus occupied, Poston had an important decision to make. Where was he to locate the headquarters of this new company? He could not choose a place where the lives of the men or the valuable property, which had been hauled from such a long distance, would be risked. The surrounding areas abounded in Apache Indians. He needed a place that could be easily defended and still be in close proximity to mining operations.

He chose Tubac, located some 50 miles south of Tucson. It had a presidio which had been abandoned by the Spanish. Tubac was nestled in a rich valley at the base of the Santa Rita Mountains. Poston knew from his first land grant expedition into Arizona that these mountains harbored old Spanish and Mexican mines.

Poston and his men went to work cleaning up the crumbling adobe fort, repairing buildings and corrals, replacing windows and doors. Some of the men were sent into the nearby forest to cut lumber for furniture. Others planted vegetable gardens. In a short while, Tubac had come to life and afforded its new occupants a comfortable living style. Now the men devoted their energy to finding and opening up the mines of the area. Soon silver deposits were bringing in over a hundred dollars a day. When the immensely rich Heintzelman Mine was discovered in Arivaca, riches began to pour into the new community.

Such activity did not go unnoticed and soon skillful Mexican miners were arriving in great numbers to find work in the new enterprise. By Christmas of that year, Poston discovered that he was in charge of a flourishing community of over a thousand people. Others might have been overwhelmed by such a burden of leadership, but not Charles Poston. The challenge of creating a utopian community which would be at once vigorous yet leisurely and filled with hope for the future was one he relished. Good meals and good conversation were the standard of the community. Young Mexican senoritas, who had come to the settlement in hopes of finding husbands, were a civilizing influence on the rough-and-tumble miners. After a day's work, music and festivities were a part of the lifestyle.

Poston even had paper money, redeemable in silver, printed for the community, which helped to ease the day-to-day transactions for necessaries. Since many of the settlers working for the company spoke only Spanish and many of the miners hired by Poston spoke a series of European languages, Poston devised a simple scheme for recognizing the value of this currency. Each bill had a picture of an animal to help designate its value. Twenty-five cents was represented by a calf, a rooster was fifty cents, a horse was a dollar and the picture of a lion was valued at $10.

Poston, as a virtual dictator in this community, used his power with generosity and kindness. He officiated at weddings and christenings, ever mindful to make the occasion one of celebration. He granted divorces and had the power to execute criminals and to declare war. So many of the community were grateful to him for his official sanctions that many young children were named after him. People flocked to Tubac. It was considered a safe, thriving place to live, and the place where a couple could easily get married.

The community flourished for several years in peace and harmony. Only once, when a priest came to investigate the

A "boleta" used by Poston as a medium of exchange at Tubac.
This one was valued at fifty cents.
(Courtesy Arizona Historical Society Library, Tucson)

religious status of the inhabitants and proceeded to declare all the marriages and the baptisms at which Poston officiated invalid, did the situation in Tubac become tense. Couples, many of whom identified with the Catholic church, began to realize that their relationships were without legal standing. Poston, with his usual skill in persuasion and in cultivating friendships, was able to persuade the priest to redo all the previous ceremonies for an agreed-upon sum, thus making them binding in the eyes of the church.

Production of silver and copper was climbing and the company expected that it would soon be earning about $3,000 a day. Poston wrote in one of his reports that he felt Tubac embodied the highest aims in human endeavor. "Full employment, not only for wealth but also for the purpose of creating a place of freedom and civilization in the territory, should serve as an example to the rest of the nation. Our experiment must elicit nothing but pride and admiration."

But the bubble of euphoria was about to burst. Due to the irresponsibility of settlers in the surrounding areas and the military stationed at a nearby fort, several incidents occurred. This resulted in the reasonably peaceful local Apaches taking to the warpath under the leadership of Cochise to avenge the wrongful deaths of several of their chiefs. The Mexicans south of the border also rose up in arms over what they viewed as blatant acts of aggression and injustice. Add to this the beginning of the Civil War and the recall of a garrison of soldiers stationed in the area for protection and Tubac was left sandwiched between angry Mexicans and Apaches with no military back-up. Poston's brother, John, was one of the first victims killed in an attack on the Heinzelman Mine.

Tubac had to be abandoned. Women and children were rushed to safety in Tucson. Thus ended the prosperity and joy of this grand experiment in community living for which so many had committed their lives and money. More than a million dollars in stores and machinery, homes and supplies had to be abandoned to destruction. The little farms that had taken hold around the community soon reverted back to desert. Poston wrote at the time that the loneliest sound he had ever heard was the crowing of the cocks on the deserted ranches. "The very chickens seemed to know that they were being forsaken."[1]

After returning home to Kentucky, Poston became involved in the movement to split the New Mexican territory, separate the western half, and create a new territory. The settlers in the Arizona half felt that the seat of the territorial government in Mesilla was too far removed from them to effectively give them adequate and protective support. Even the leaders of the New Mexico territory were anxious to eliminate the burden of having to deal with the Apache problem. But each time the bill came before Congress it was defeated because of other pending problems, such as the issue of whether slavery should be allowed in the new territory. The situation dragged on and on. Each new petition was rejected because of another Congressional disagreement.

By now the Civil War was in full fury. Congress was looking for ways to fund this exceedingly expensive war. What was needed was a new source of gold and silver to infuse into the military in hopes of bringing this destructive war to a quick resolution. Heintzelman, by now a general in the Union army, had the ear of President Abraham Lincoln. Here was a perfect opportunity to once again bring before Congress the mineral potential of Arizona and the need to forge closer ties with the area by creating it as a separate territory.

General Heintzelman recalled the magical enthusiasm that Poston could bring to a speech. In Heintzelman's mind, Charles Poston was that perfect combination of talents to successfully take up Arizona's cause in Congress. Poston had much firsthand knowledge of the area. He personally knew of the mineral wealth, but most of all he had that ability to persuade and charm, to create with words a vivid vision, a dream of the potential of the place.

General Heintzelman set up a meeting with Poston and his fellow Kentuckian, President Abraham Lincoln. The President listened carefully and then sent Poston to men who had the power to get a bill creating an Arizona territory through the Congress. Once again Charles Poston, with his natural ability as promoter, raconteur and visionary, used those talents to persuade these powerful political men. On February 24, 1863, the results of Poston's persuasive abilities came to fruition, and President Abraham Lincoln signed a bill creating the Arizona Territory.

A jubilant Poston invited these new friends and political colleagues, who had worked for the success of the bill, to a celebration dinner. As the evening progressed, the wily politicians began to parcel out the jobs and positions that this new territory had created. Poston, even though host and catalyst, was ignored. Astounded by this blatant disinterest in rewarding him for his labors, Poston fortified himself with several glasses of wine and exclaimed to his assembled guests, "Well, gentlemen, what is to become of me?"[2]

Eventually he was offered the office of Superintendent of Indian Affairs. This was not a powerful nor lucrative position, but it did give Poston his opportunity to return to his beloved Arizona.

Having outfitted himself and his party in what was by now his personal style of comfortable travel, Poston, armed with many gifts for the Indians, invited a friend from San Francisco to join him on his journey through Arizona as he visited the various Indian tribes. It might be easy to dismiss the skill of Charles Poston as superintendent of the Indians because of his penchant for luxury, drama and good times, but he was and had always been a keen observer of the precarious conditions under which the Indians lived. Their living style was to be in even greater peril because of the rapid encroachment by settlers on their hunting, farming and foraging lands. The visionary, the dreamer, did much in the way of coming up with constructive ideas to better the lives of the Indians.

Poston also knew how to use the skills of others to give his plans a firm foundation. He hired an engineer to help him create a plan for a proposed Indian reservation along the Colorado River, which would make use of canal irrigation for fertilizing the farmland. By developing an irrigation program, he was making certain that the Indians would be able to be self-sufficient in supplying themselves with food, but it would be done in a manner that was based on a successful irrigation system told about in the familiar Indian tales of the ancient ones from a time long ago.

Poston was able to persuade the territorial legislature to agree with the proposal. Then he ran for the office of territorial delegate to Congress. This would allow him to personally present his proposals for the Indians. As a delegate, Poston presented more than 10 resolutions concerning the needs of this fledgling territory. In addition, he gave eloquent speeches in support of his Indian programs. Much of his vision did not interest the men in Washington, D.C. Few had the foresight to see the Indians as anything more than savages to be ignored or eliminated. Some token bills were passed which gave small amounts of money for incidental expenses, such as supplying the Indians with farming equipment, but without the canals of irrigation, the money was a mere assuaging of conscience.

Three years after Poston's plea for the Indians, Congress did pass a bill setting up a small reservation with the start of some irrigation construction. It was better than nothing, but had Poston's vision for the Indians been followed, perhaps much of the hate and tragedy that occurred in Arizona between the settlers and the native Americans might have been averted.

But, long-range visions are not the stuff of politics. In what appeared to be some political collusion, Poston found himself in a three-way contest for re-election as territorial delegate to Congress. All three candidates ran on the same ticket and

Poston lost.

Returning to Washington, where he began to practice law, Poston still hoped to realize his political ambitions. He had become a friend of President Lincoln and was viewed in Washington as a man who had the right connections and influence. All this came to an abrupt end some few months later with the assassination of the President. Without his fellow Kentuckian's support, there was little call for Poston's services.

Returning to Arizona, he tried once again to be the successful candidate for delegate to Congress. Again he was defeated. Rejected by a place that meant so much to him, the relentless Poston went to Europe and wrote a book about his experiences. Returning to Washington, Poston was commissioned by the Secretary of State to go to Asia to study irrigation and immigration.

Everything about Asia fascinated him. Armed with a treaty to the Emperor of China and many letters of introduction, he met not only the Emperor, but the Mikado of Japan, the Viceroy of India, the Khedive of Egypt, the Sultan of Turkey, the Shah of Persia and the Kings and Queens of Europe. Much later, he was to remark that none of those great leaders embodied the majesty of humanity that he had found in Abraham Lincoln.

While in India, Poston was to discover the Parsees and their ancient Zoroastrian religion. These were the Sunworshippers who believed in the prophet Zoroaster, who had lived one thousand years before Christ, and espoused the continuing universal struggle between the forces of light and darkness. The Parsees fascinated Poston with their belief that man can choose to take part in the struggle against the elements of darkness by worshipping and supporting the Lord of Light, who is eternally engaged in the battle against the forces of evil.

Poston was so taken by this religion and the study of its history and temples that he was accused of neglecting the study of ditches and irrigation. When Washington heard about Poston's use of time, his commission was withdrawn. Poston continued his travels, supporting himself by writing articles about his experiences. For awhile he lived in England, where he wrote a book about his new-found religion. His charm, his vision, his enthusiasm opened many doors and Poston was sought after as a speaker and writer. Still desirous of holding political office, Poston decided to return to Washington. But his political ambitions were to bear no fruit.

With a sick wife in Washington, Poston needed a source of steady income. Although he was a man who had met and known the rich and famous of the world, the only appointment that was offered him was the position of Register of Land in Florence, Arizona. Florence had a population of 500 when Poston arrived. He worked in a small adobe room at a modest salary and was to remain there for the next four lonely years. There was little to interest a man who had lived in such exciting capitals as Washington, D.C., and London. He wrote a book. He took to exploring the area.

One day he noticed a hill whose shape was reminiscent of an Egyptian pyramid. On that hill he found the ruins of a stone tower. Poston began to wonder if those ruins were not the product of some ancient Indians, the forebears of the Hohokam, perhaps even the Aztecs, who had brought the religion of Zoroaster and the worship of the sun to Florence thousands of years ago.

If this was so, perhaps the fates had brought him back to Arizona, to this tiny insignificant place, because of his knowledge of that eastern religion. Was he meant to discover, to recreate, to bring back to full flourishing the ancient practices of Sunworshipping? He built a road up to the tower on the hill at his own expense. He wrote to the Shah of Persia to enlist his help in recreating in this Arizona desert a temple to the Shah's ancestors who worshipped Zoroaster. He wrote articles publicizing his findings, hoping to encourage those who might wish to follow this religion and help support his efforts.

He entertained in a home he had built beside his hill. He invited all his friends to come and celebrate his vision. He would build a temple of the sun at the apex of the hill. Champagne was drunk, gourmet food was eaten, fireworks lit up the midnight sky, the flag to the sun was raised, a new community of worshippers was to begin.

But funds were not forthcoming. The Parsees showed little interest in a temple in a distant desert far across an ocean. His ability to excite others with his vision waned. It was too strange a dream, too mystifying, too far outside the realism of life in Arizona. Discouraged, he resigned from the land office commission.

The next years of Poston's life found him employed as a customs officer at various settlements along the Mexican border. At one point, he was placed in charge of an agricultural experiment station in Phoenix. But the promise of his early opportunities brought nothing more than a slow and steady decline in prestige, position and the acquisition of money.

Arizona, the place he had helped to birth, gradually forgot about him in his old age. He would eventually live in Phoenix in near squalor until the legislature, having become aware of his straitened circumstances, presented him with a modest pension of $25 a month.

Charles Poston died in June of 1902. At 75 years of age, he was totally alone. The Father of Arizona had been forgotten by all. His body lay unclaimed in Phoenix as attempts were made to locate relatives. Burial in the local potters' field seemed to be imminent. Then the editor of the *Arizona Republican* wrote an article asking the pioneers and citizens of Phoenix to help. Hundreds offered to help in the funeral arrangements.

Twenty-three years after his death, the citizens of Arizona decided to honor the man whose own life was so completely intertwined with Arizona's history. What more fitting honor could be bestowed than to acknowledge his last great vision. A small stone pyramid tomb was created on top of his peaceful hill in Florence. His remains were transferred there. Now Charles Poston can forever rest in the sun that shines so steadily on the land he helped to establish.

[1]Poston, Charles "Building a State in Apache Land, War-Time in Arizona," *Overland Monthly,* September 1894, Volume XXIV, Number 141, page 296.
[2]Poston, Charles, "Building a State in Apache Land, Concluded," *Overland Monthly,* October 1894, Volume XXVI, Number 42, Second Series, Page 404.

BIBLIOGRAPHY
Gressinger, A. W., *Charles Poston, Sunland Seer*, Dale Stuart King, Publisher, Globe, Arizona, 1961.
Hall, Sharlot, "The Father of Arizona," *Arizona, The New State Magazine*, Volume II, Number 10, Phoenix, Arizona, August 1912.
Poston, Charles D., "Building a State in Apache Land," four articles, *Overland Monthly*, July 1894, August 1894, September 1894, October 1894, Volume XXVI, Numbers 39-42, Overland Publishing Company, San Francisco. Edited by Rounsevelle Wildman.
Smith, Dale, "Sonoran Camelot," *Arizona Trend*, Volume 3, Number 12, Phoenix, Arizona, August 1989.
Wagoner, Jay J., *Arizona's Heritage*, Peregrine Smith, Inc., Santa Barbara and Salt Lake City, 1977.

Slim Woman and the Navajos

Many years ago, Slim Woman came to the land of the Navajos. It was a strange, beautiful desert land, filled with big red rocks and great, wide, sky-blue places. Slim Woman was only two years old when she arrived in the Southwest, a child of a pioneer family called the Wades. Her family called her Louisa. At night, her mother put little Louisa's bed on the floor of the cabin below the window, safe from Indian bullets. When she woke up at night there was always the shadow of the guard and his gun. Little Louisa knew they were not safe from the Indians. She knew of their anger at these settlers, who had come to stay and to fence in their Indian land.

Slim Woman loved this land of desert, mountain and meadow. She enjoyed picking wildflowers for her mother. As a little girl, she remembered not only her mother's pleasure in receiving her gift but also her constant words of caution. "Louisa, never wander far from the house. Children have been kidnapped and killed by the Indians." Later, Slim Woman was to remember how she had hidden behind her mother's skirts when friendly Navajos came to the farm. Later Slim Woman would laugh at those early childish fears, for the Indians were to become her friends, her people.

The Wade family was a part of that river of settlers who flowed unceasingly across the continent. They chose to settle in a mountainous area near the southwestern tip of Colorado next to the Mancos River. It was there that Louisa Wade grew to be a slim, lively teenager. She worked hard at all the household tasks that frontier girls did, but whenever there was time, she would go to the dances of the small farming community. She would join any gathering where there was the promise of some group singing. She loved being on a horse and never missed a chance to join friends for a Sunday afternoon ride. Often John would come too. John was the son of a neighboring farmer. He was a quiet, kindly Quaker who was attracted to Louisa's fun-loving ways.

Now there had been cowboys in from the range for her to choose among for a husband, and there had been the boys from her high school, but in her heart there had always been John Wetherill. How wonderful it was to watch him ride, so tall and at ease in the saddle. John, more than any other man she knew, told her wonderful stories about the places he had explored as a boy and as a young man, the hidden trails that led to canyons where there were mysterious Indian buildings. He told her about the Desert People with their flocks of sheep, who wandered in this vast and empty land.

The more John told her, the greater became her desire to see these places for herself. She wanted to visit the part of this country where there were no white men. She wanted to see their hogans, the dwelling places of these Navajos, who dressed in velvet blouses and wore lovely silver jewelry. How she wished to know that land of wind and searing light, of great high rocks and shining moonlit water.

In 1896, after a year's engagement, Louisa Wade, full of bright courage, married John Wetherill. It was the beginning of a marriage that was to last a lifetime. It would be this couple's destiny to discover astounding ancient Indian ruins, as well as one of the greatest natural wonders of the world. Eventually they would be recognized as the first pioneers who saw the need to understand and preserve the complex and wonderful culture of the Navajo people of Arizona. Louisa Wade Wetherill's curiosity about the Navajos was to culminate in her becoming a vital and necessary link between two cultures whose lifestyles and goals were alien to each other.

The first years of their marriage were filled with hard times. Louisa and John tried to follow in their parents' footsteps and earn their living by farming. Success eluded them. One year, the crops died from not enough rain. Another year, the cold killed the crops before they were ready for harvest. Then disease destroyed still more. During this time, a son, Benjamin, was born and then Georgia, a daughter. The farm could not produce enough for the young family to survive. All their hard work had accomplished nothing. They had to find another way to earn their livelihood.

It was John's brother who suggested that they start a trading post for the Indians. "The Navajos need coffee, flour, sugar and supplies," he said. "They will trade beautifully-woven blankets, skins and lovely necklaces and bracelets made of silver." Would it be safe? wondered Louisa. Did they really have a choice? What was preferable: slowly dying of starvation or being finished off in a quick raid? They would have to take the chance. They had to try something. So, in 1900, the young couple undertook the management of their first Navajo trading post. This began a 45-year journey of being with the Navajos, living with them, learning from them and growing to love them.

At first, even a frontier girl like Louisa was not prepared for how hard a life it was, trying to run a trading post far from the community of her youth. The Indian lands of New Mexico near Gallup were very isolated from all white people. Often her husband would be gone for days and weeks at a time, getting supplies or guiding scientists to newly-discovered ancient Indian ruins.

At this time, her son was only four years old; her daughter was just two. Her 16-year-old brother was her only companion and protection when John was away. Constantly she was surrounded by these strange Indians speaking only their own odd-sounding language. She could not understand them. They kept their distance from her. Yet she soon lost her fear of these wandering people, these skillful artisans who moved silently in and out of the trading post. The days while John was away blended one into another. It was a dream-like time. There were chores to do, the children to take care of, the trading to be accomplished.

At first the only words Louisa learned were the Navajo trade words, the words for numbers, blankets, silver, bracelet, goat-skin, coffee and sugar. At first she saw no reason to learn more.

Then one day, not long after they had settled, her brother became ill. Louisa shuddered with fear as she recognized the signs of pneumonia. John was on an expedition at least 70 miles away. She was alone with two little children and a brother sick with a disease that often resulted in death.

She tried to communicate with the Navajos her need for help. Her trade words proved useless. They did not understand her directions for finding her husband or getting the necessary medicines. They became embarrassed at her tears and trembling face and moved their families to a respectful distance from the trading post. There they sat and waited for whatever fate would bring. And so the nightmare began: completely-surrounded by

Louisa Wade Wetherill
(Courtesy of the Wetherill Family Collection)

Navajo people, she was desperately and totally alone.

A few days later, two white men rode into the trading post. "Please," she begged them, "stay here, I've no one to help me."

"We're no good at nursing the sick, ma'am," they said, "and we're pushing hard to cover the miles to where we need to go."

Nothing she said could persuade them to stay. They did finally promise to take a letter to her father and mother asking them to come. But it would take so long for a letter to be delivered, she despaired at getting help in time.

Each night she sat exhausted by her brother's bed and watched him getting weaker and weaker. Louisa, only 22 years old, felt overwhelmed. It was too much, too hard to handle all alone. Frustrated, angry tears poured down her face as she realized that she wasn't alone. She was completely surrounded by a people who did not understand what she so desperately wanted to communicate. They did not understand what she needed.

Then one night, when things looked completely hopeless, she heard the sound of a wagon. Out of that cold winter night came a white trader she knew. "I've never been so glad to see anyone in my life," she cried. "I think my brother is dying and there's been no one here to help me."

The trader, realizing that Louisa was very near collapse, stayed with her. He managed to explain to the Indians the directions and urgency for getting to her husband. In a few days, her husband and parents arrived. They brought medicine and soon her brother began to get well.

For Louisa Wetherill, that experience was a turning point in her life. Never again would she allow herself to be so helpless, so alone. She made a promise then and there that she would learn the language of the Navajos; she would make them her friends. From now on, no matter how far she was from a white settlement, as long as she was among the Navajo Indians, the barrier of language would never again isolate her from them.

She found an old Indian woman who spoke some English. It was not an easy task she had set for herself. Navajo is a difficult language. Each change of tone, each change of breath gives new meaning to a word. In fact the Navajo language is so complicated that it was successfully used as a code language during both World Wars. In time Louisa began to learn and to understand.

The Indians were soon astonished with her skill. No white person, certainly no white woman had ever learned to speak Navajo so well, for the language was replete with allegory and poetic allusion. Was it possible for such a thing to happen? Some thought that she could not learn their style of speaking that quickly if she were totally white. Many began to believe that she must have some Navajo blood or the spirit of some long lost Indian woman in her to be able to speak with such ease. The Navajos began to feel that she must be one of the People herself. They called her Slim Woman, *Asthon Sosi*, in their language. They began to trust her, to tell her of their lives.

Slim Woman was captivated with all she heard and saw. What a fascinating people were these Navajos! She admired the dignity and kindness which they brought to their lives. She found herself thinking more and more like them, understanding them, sympathizing with their chosen way of life. She loved to sit and listen to their stories, particularly the children's stories which not only told how to recognize animals, but with great subtlety and gentle humor told of the acceptable ways of behaving in living one's life. Sometimes she would share her feelings about these Indians with her gentle Quaker husband. "John, many of the settlers have treated these people with great carelessness and selfishness. They have not tried to understand."

For the next five years, John and Louisa Wetherill worked at various trading posts in the northwestern section of New Mexico, never with particular financial success. But, they managed to make a living. They were learning. John became a skillful guide to an endless stream of scientists who were suddenly coming from all over the world to view the half-forgotten ruins of the ancient people, to marvel at the complexity of these lost civilizations, to ponder the mystery of why they had disappeared.

Then John and Louisa decided to penetrate even deeper into this isolated land. They planned to move to Arizona, to Oljato, the Indian name for the place of moonlight water, near the great valley of monuments. At first John and Louisa's brother were to go alone and scout the area, for they had heard rumors that the Indians there were hostile. If conditions were found to be acceptable, Louisa and the children would make the move. But, the Indians told them they could not come this far into their land. "Turn back," said Hoskinini-begay, son of the chief, for they were weary of the white people who had rounded up so many of their clan, forcing them to march to a place in New Mexico far from their homes. There, in Bosque Redondo, many had died.

John Wetherill, so gentle in his Quaker ways, proposed instead that the Indians join him and partake in a rabbit feast. Surprised by the offer of sharing food, the Indians agreed. At the feast, John gave them coffee and sugar and baked bread from his supplies of flour. He missed Louisa's skill at their language as he haltingly explained to Hoskinini's people that these were some of the supplies that they could provide to the tribe. At last, when the feast was done, John Wetherill was given permission to continue the journey, to go to Kayenta, the moonlight's water, to go into the land where clouds and flocks of sheep drift in peace.

It was in this compelling Monument Valley that John and Louisa were to remain for the greater part of their lives. Relatives of Slim Woman say they often remember her sitting under a tree in the summer with as many as a hundred Indians about her, listening to the stories, laughing and talking as happily as anyone there. The Navajos had accepted Louisa as one of their own. She was called granddaughter by Chief Hoskinini. The old ones of the tribe called her daughter and sister. The young called her mother.

But the great adventures of their journey to this land had only just begun. John could now begin to do the type of exploring that he had done as a young man and boy. Whenever he could, he would investigate this vast unknown region surrounding the now-established trading post. He was happiest when he could take a horse and a few supplies and wander, viewing a country never before seen by white man since the time of the Spanish explorers.

Years before, his brother had been the first white man to see the huge silent apartment dwellings of the Mesa Verde in Colorado. Soon after that, John visited those great ruins. The mystery of those silent houses touched feelings deep within him. He felt certain there were other forgotten houses of the Old People to be found in hidden canyons. Louisa agreed with him. She told him of the legends she had heard which mentioned other ancient dwellings, as well as bones of giant animals. John was determined to find all of this, to learn all he could about these people who had disappeared so very long ago.

The quiet Quaker systematically began to search the many canyons and hidden recesses of this fascinating land. Everytime he returned to the trading post, he would share with Louisa all that he had seen. His wanderings eventually led him to discover many pueblo ruins, as well as one of the finest ancient Indian communal dwellings built in a huge cliff cave to be found anywhere in Arizona.

At first John came upon a place the Indians called Keet Seel, the native term for "broken pottery." John's brother had discovered these ruins some years previously, but had had no time to investigate further. This village of the lost Old Ones had rooms for 500 people. Hundreds and hundreds of years ago, this had been a thriving, artistically gifted community who had made beautiful pottery. Then the inhabitants simply disap-

Louisa Wade Wetherill with Sam Chief and family
(Courtesy of the Wetherill Family Collection)

peared. Sandals, clothing and household items were left as if there had been no other plan than to return shortly. John, with a scientist's care, took photographs, made drawings and carefully preserved all he discovered. Louisa and the children joined him on these expeditions and marveled at the mysterious beauty of this home of the Ancient Ones.

John could barely breathe when he first peered across a canyon and sighted Betatakin. This forgotten pueblo was set in a cave over 500 feet wide, 150 feet deep and 400 feet high. The Indians could tell him little about the Old Clan who had lived there. Why had they left? Were they worn out by a long struggle against the Water God who breathed hot fire which dried up lakes and streams and took away the rain? Had some strange disease forced them to seek other places to live? Were there no clues as to what had happened to those Old People who had come from this land which changes and yet somehow remains changeless?

Louisa knew of the Navajo legend which told of great droughts which lasted many years and a decline in the vitality of the clan by too much isolation and intermarriage. Blindness and disease weakened them. For Slim Woman, the story and the ruin were a window into another time, another life.

Every day brought to Louisa Wade Wetherill some new learning, some new discovery about the Navajos. She collected over 300 different herbs that they used. She meticulously described which were used for foods, for medicines and for sacred ceremonies. She listened and listened to their stories.

Then one day she heard a story that was to bring this couple notoriety beyond anything they could have conceived. For some time, John had been intrigued with rock formations that formed small arches and bridges and which could be seen in some of the canyons.

"John," she said, "I have just heard from one of the Navajos a most fascinating story about a huge rock bridge. He says the stone bridge is as large and as tall as a rainbow."

John speculated as he listened to Louisa tell the story. Did the story have a basis of truth? Could there ever be a rock arch as large as a rainbow?

"Once, a long time ago, there was a young chieftain out hunting alone in the canyons. A rain storm came so fast and furiously that the desert land could not soak up the water. The land began to flood with raging, turbulent water. The young chieftain knew that a person caught in such a flood would most surely drown.

Quickly the young man began to climb to higher ground. But the waters continued to rise higher and higher. At last he was at the top of a knoll of land. All around him was swirling water. There was nowhere else for him to climb. Across the water some 300 feet away was a tall mountain-like cliff. He knew if he could somehow get there he would be safe. But the water was too swift for him to swim. The cliff was too far for him to jump. Had he but a rope, he could shoot it across with his arrow and swing himself across. But he had no rope.

Soon he felt the water lapping at his moccasins. And he began to pray the prayer of the lost. He began to chant to the North Wind to send him a rainbow, that he might climb it and cross the water in peace.

But the water continued to rise. The young chieftain continued to pray and chant to each of the spirit winds, the South Wind, the East Wind, the West Wind. Always his prayer was the same: send me a rainbow so that I might cross the raging waters in peace.

As the water reached the young man's chest, a swirling mist descended and surrounded him. The winds began to blow and howl. Through the mist, he could see a beautiful rainbow being formed. Before his eyes he watched as the transparent rainbow began to harden into a lovely pink rock bridge. With a desperate lunge, the young chief pulled himself up onto the rainbow bridge and crossed over the turbulent water beneath him to safety and peace."

When Slim Woman finished the story, they remained silent, still under the spell of the words. Then Louisa spoke softly but with great excitement, "The Indians say that there is such a place, John, a very sacred place where there is a large rock rainbow that still remains to this day."

Louisa and John believed the story. They began to ask about the possible location of this rainbow rock. No one knew where it was; the location had been lost somewhere in the telling. Then one day, a visiting Indian from another area said that he had personally seen it once long ago when he was a young boy. He and his cousin had been trying to capture some wild horses and

Rainbow Bridge at Lake Powell, the world's largest known natural bridge, 309 feet high (Courtesy Arizona Office of Tourism)

had wandered far into canyons where they had never been before. In the distance, they saw an enormous rainbow of rock.

With help from this Indian as his guide, John was eventually able to find what is now considered one of the great natural wonders of the world, the Rainbow Bridge, located just north of the Arizona border.

When Rainbow Bridge was dedicated as a national monument, it was Louisa Wetherill, Slim Woman, who insisted that the plaque honoring the person who discovered the great natural wonder should name the Indian guide who had led John to the discovery of it. Louisa also insisted that the dedication ceremony include the praying of the sacred chant of the lost that she first heard in that wonderful Native American story. For it was the myths and legends which she helped to preserve that gave the Navajos some sense of security during those times when their world was changing far, far too quickly and many lost their balance as they struggled to live between two disparate societies.

In those early times and perhaps still today, it is rare to find an individual who is able to develop an empathy and a sensitive understanding for a culture such as that of the Navajos. Louisa Wade Wetherill was such a person. The Indians so trusted her that many times they brought their arguments to Slim Woman to settle. Serious-faced Indians would come from miles away to sit in her dining room or in front of her house to explain their problems and to accept her decisions. She had the reputation for being honest and fair. Often her decisions reflected a deep awareness of the mental process of these people which few Indian agents hired by the government ever even attempted to achieve.

One time there was an argument over a cow which belonged to a Navajo and was killed by some young Paiute boys.

"She was a good, young cow," said the Navajo and his family, "she was the best one we ever had."

The father of the Paiute boys disagreed. "She was a very old cow, long past her prime. She was not worth anything."

For nearly three hours, 30 Navajos and Paiutes sat in Slim Woman's house arguing. In their midst, Louisa listened carefully to every opinion. A resolution seemed no closer after hours of argument. The Indians turned to her, *"Asthon Sosi,"* they said, "you must show us the way to an answer, for we see no way but fighting."

The Navajo stood up, there was anger in his stance. "Give me a horse for the cow and we will shake hands."

"No," answered the Paiute, contempt in his voice, "the cow is not worth a horse."

Slim Woman realized that no agreement was going to be reached. The tension in the room was palpable. She raised her hand. Everyone in the room turned toward her. She began to speak quietly, "Some time ago, I lost my colt. Some of you helped look for him. You found his bones at the foot on the mountain. Remember, you told me that you knew the bones belonged to a horse that was young and fat because the bones were yellow. If it had been a thin, old horse the bones would have been white. Now if this is true and I think it must be, I will tell you how to settle this argument."

Every eye was upon Slim Woman. The silence was complete. "We will select one Navajo and one Paiute to go and get the bones of the cow. If the bones are yellow, the cow was fat and the Paiute will give the Navajo a horse for his loss. If the bones are white, nothing more needs to be done."

A sigh rippled through the assembly of Indians. Everyone agreed with Slim Woman's plan.

Suddenly, the father of the Paiute boys stood up. "You need not send for the bones," he said. "I will give you the horse."

Again and again it was repeated in the hogans, "Slim Woman has wisdom." The Indians trusted their *Asthon Sosi.*

By now Louisa was more than skilled in the slow desert speech of the Navajo. She had somehow learned to recognize the poetry of their language and the deep spiritual foundation of their lives. More and more, she came to realize the sensitivity and awareness of the Native American mind.

In time, the clan allowed Slim Woman to witness a ceremony that they had never before allowed a white person to see and experience. Louisa was given the honor of watching the ceremony of healing and the creation of the sand painting of healing. Never before had she seen such beautiful colors of sand or such elaborate drawings as those used to cure the ill. When the ceremony was over the sand drawing was gathered up and thrown northward upon the desert to be released, gone and lost forever.

Although she understood that the sand was used to take on the illness and the painting was destroyed to dispel the malady, Louisa was saddened by the loss of such exquisite artwork. How she wanted some memory of those lovely, colorful drawings made with colored sand! It took a long time to overcome the hesitancy of the medicine men before she was able to achieve the trust of two of them, Yellow Singer and Wolfkiller. Yellow Singer eventually became willing to reproduce some of the drawings for her with crayons. For Slim Woman, he would do it. They knew that she would honor their sacred sand paintings. Because of their trust in her, today we are able to have copies of the beautiful Navajo paintings of sand.

Patiently, hour after hour, filling up boxes upon boxes of files, Louisa recorded the stories, the legends, the chants of her Indian friends. Many of her collections can now be found in the libraries of our Arizona universities.

During the nearly 40 years that Slim Woman and her husband lived at the trading post in Kayenta, Arizona, thousands of visitors, many scholars from museums and universities, many famous and renowned people such as Zane Grey, John Houston and a former President, Teddy Roosevelt, came to accept the Wetherill hospitality and to go with John to see the great Indian ruins and natural wonders that were near their home. But, when they were done with those grand outdoor journeys, they came back to the trading post and stayed to listen to Slim Woman tell the stories of the Navajos and to receive from her tantalizing glimpses into the fascinating lives of these people.

By the early 1920s, Slim Woman and John, still living so far from civilization in the heart of the land of the Navajos, were known throughout the world. Louisa Wade Wetherill was invited to give talks about her life among the Navajos all over the West.

Louisa Wetherill lived to be 68 years old. She died on September 18, 1945, about one year after the death of her beloved husband. She was a pioneer who became a mother to the Navajos. When she came to Arizona, Louisa helped make it a better place by genuinely caring about its native people. Today she is still remembered for her prodigious and thoughtful work

Louisa with daughter Georgia Ida
(Courtesy of the Wetherill Family Collection)

among the Navajos. She has been given honorable recognition by the state of Arizona and has had her named placed in the Arizona Women's Hall of Fame.

BIBLIOGRAPHY

Comfort, May Apoline, *Rainbow to Yesterday, the John and Louisa Wetherill Story*, Vantage Press, New York, 1980.

Crowe, Rosalie and Tod, Diane, *Arizona Women's Hall of Fame*, Arizona Historical Society Museum Monograph, Central Arizona Division, Phoenix, Arizona, 1985.

Mazza, Evelyn M., telephone conversation and letter, 1987.

Wagoner, Jay J., *Arizona's Heritage*, Peregrine Smith, Inc., Santa Barbara and Salt Lake City, 1977.

Wetherill, Louisa Wade, "Navaho Recipes," "Story of the First Lie," "The Woman Whose Nose Was Cut Off Twelve Times," *Kiva*, Volume XII, March 1947, pages 25-39.

Wetherill, Louisa and Gillmor, Frances, *Traders to the Navajos*, Houghton Mifflin, New York, 1934, University of New Mexico Press, 1953 and 1965 (paperback).

Wetherill, Lulu W. and Cummings, Byron, "A Navaho Folk Tale of Pueblo Bonito," *Art and Archeology*, 1922, Vol. XIV, page 132.

The Mystery of the Lady in Blue

Three hundred and fifty years ago, when Spanish explorers and missionaries first entered the Southwest, they found an untamed land, and tribes of unknown people whose baffling culture and way of life they sought to change. They expected to witness the unusual, but even they were not prepared for encounters with Indians who already knew of the "white man" and his religion from visits with a beautiful white woman dressed in blue.

In those olden days, these Spanish explorers and missionaries were the first Europeans who had ever explored the Southwest. They were an aggressive and arrogant group of men who looked upon the desert as a dreary, barren wasteland and the natives as a species of beings less than human. Often they would laugh among themselves, saying that only men such as themselves, and horses could survive in this harsh land; women and dogs would never live long.

Yet time and again, the journals written by the missionaries during 1629 to 1631 tell of sightings by the Indians of a young, beautiful, white woman dressed in a flowing gown of blue.

The first written account we have comes from the journal of a Father Alonzo de Benavides. At that time, Fray Alonzo was in charge of several missions in the Southwest. He wrote:

> One day, a strange delegation of Indians came to our mission. I had never seen them before. With the help of our interpreter, the Indians told us that they had come from far over the mountains, from an area our missionaries had never before explored. I asked them what they wanted. They were quite savage-looking, yet when our interpreter explained their request, we were puzzled.
>
> These strange Indians desired a priest to accompany them and return with them to their village to baptize everyone in their tribe. They also wanted a padre to help them build a church. Suspicious of their motive, I asked them why should they wish this. They answered that they had learned all about our Christian God and wished to worship him. Still very perplexed, I asked them how they had heard of our work here at the mission. "Oh," they answered, "it was the beautiful, young white lady dressed in a flowing gown of blue. She came to our village and, speaking in our language, told us all about your Christian god. She also told us to come to the mission here."

"Well, where did the lady come from?" I asked. "We don't know," they answered. "One day she just appeared." I persisted, "Well, where did she go?" The Indians shook their heads bewildered and said, "She just disappeared."

"The Indians remained with us at the mission for several days while we readied a priest to return with them. Among our possessions at the mission was a painting of the sister of one of our men. When the Indians saw the picture, they cried out excitedly, "That is old lady, our lady is very young lady, but she is wearing the same kind of dress." The woman in the picture was wearing a nun's habit and was a mother superior of a convent in Spain. This strange experience happened to me once again with a different tribe, yet their story was essentially the same.

Father Alonzo decided to write to Spain to find out whether the religious authorities were now sending women over as missionaries. After many months, he received a reply stating that no women were being sent to the Southwest. At this time, no women were being sent to the New World for any reason.

Some years later, a Father Damien Manzanet, who was in charge of a mission near the Texas border, recorded in his journal the following incident. "A chief from a neighboring tribe came to me wanting to trade vegetables and skins for a piece of blue cloth. In the course of our bartering, I asked him what he wanted to do with the material. He said, 'My mother is getting very old and will soon die. When she dies, we want to wrap her in the blue cloth.' I tried to explain to the chief that he did not want blue but rather black material because black was the color for a shroud. The Indian chief shook his head very upset; he insisted that he wanted blue cloth or none. Puzzled by his determination I asked him, 'Why?' He replied that his tribe was fond of the color blue, particularly for burial clothes. 'Was there a reason for this fondness?' I asked. 'Oh yes,' he answered, 'many years ago, before I was born, when my mother was a very young girl, a beautiful, young white woman dressed in a flowing gown of blue came down from the hills to our village and, speaking in our language, told us all about your Christian god, baptized us, and helped us build a church. Since that time, we always dress those who die in blue cloth. It is our hope that they will journey to meet the lady once more.' "

A Frenchman named Saint Dennis wrote in his journal that while visiting the Southwest, he noticed a strange and perplexing custom among the Indians. "Often," he wrote, "they would

An artist's conception of Father Kino
(Courtesy Arizona Historical Society Library, Tucson)

ask for blue cloth to bury their dead. Their reason was always the same. A great many years ago, a beautiful woman had come to their village dressed all in blue and, speaking their language, had baptized everyone in the village including the medicine man. So great was the impression she had made that they wanted their dead to enter the next world dressed in blue like the woman."

The next journal entry we have comes from our very own Father Eusebio Kino, who started the missions here in southern Arizona and in the northern Sonoran area of Mexico.

Father Kino was traveling with another missionary, Father Matheo Manje, who kept a journal of their travels as they visited various Pima tribes along the Gila River.

"While we were at one of the villages," wrote Father Manje, "an old man told us the following story. 'One day, a beautiful, strange, young white lady dressed in a flowing gown of blue appeared at our village and began to speak to us in a language that we did not understand. The more she spoke, the louder she became, and soon she was shouting at us. Many of our people became frightened. Some of our warriors shot arrows at her and she collapsed onto the floor of the desert. We ran away leaving her for dead. Many hours later, when we returned to where she had been lying, she had disappeared.' The old Indian went on to say that a few days later she returned and started to yell at them once more in a strange language. Frightened, the Indians ran away."

Father Kino and his assistant doubted the truth of the Indian's story and decided to test his memory further. Had they ever seen a white person before? he asked. "Oh yes," replied the old man nodding his head vigorously. "Many years ago, before the lady in blue, a white captain on a large horse passed through our village with many soldiers and horses. He was following our river to the great river to the west and to the land beyond that."

Father Kino recognized the Indian's description. The old Indian had accurately described the famous Spanish explorer, Captain Juan de Onate, who had led an expedition to the Colorado River and on to California. Father Kino reasoned that if the old man's description of Onate was accurate, was not his story of a mysterious lady in blue also true?

So the stories found their way into the written records of the time, but always with unanswered questions. Who was this woman? Where did she come from? Where did she go? How could a single woman survive by herself in the vast Southwestern wilderness? She was never seen to take nourishment although the Indians often offered her food. How was it that she could speak several Indian languages and yet could not speak Pima? That is the mystery.

There seems to be a beginning of an answer to this mysterious puzzle. The answer begins with the later journals of Father Alonzo. After staying in the Southwest for several years, Father Alonzo returned to Spain. While traveling in Spain, he met Maria de Jesus de Agreda, a Mother Superior of her convent. Maria de Jesus came from a prominent, wealthy Spanish family and became a nun when she was just 17 years old. She was so devout and capable that the Pope, by papal dispensation, made her head of her order when she was only 25 years old. But this honor did not totally satisfy Maria. She wanted to have the challenge of doing greater things for her faith than remaining cloistered in her convent. Priests and brothers from various religious orders were being sent to the New World to preach to

Tumacacori National Monument
(Courtesy Arizona Office of Tourism)

the natives. Maria wanted the chance, the opportunity, to do the same. But in those days the Southwest was no place for a woman, particularly a young and beautiful nun.

Maria continued her peaceful and prayerful life at the convent, ministering to her sisters and to the poor, while her spirit yearned for more. Maria explained all of this to Father Alonzo during his visit to the convent at Agreda. "How much I admire you priests who are allowed to do missionary work in the New World," she told him. "I wish that I could do the same and go to those people and tell them the stories of our Jesus."

For a long while she sat quietly in front of Father Alonzo, her large black eyes lowered as if in deep thought. Finally she raised her pale face and spoke to him in the softest of whispers, "Some days when I go into my little room in the afternoon to meditate and pray, I fall into a deep sleep and I dream the most vivid dreams."

She then described her dreams to Father Alonzo, telling him she had dreamt that she was visiting the New World, the great

Southwest. Father Alonzo listened in astonishment, for Maria de Jesus was describing to him with an uncanny accuracy places he believed that only he had visited in the Southwest. For two weeks he questioned her, asking her for more and more detail of what she saw in her dreams. Maria described the dress and the homes of the Indians. Father Alonzo reacted with increasing alarm to her descriptions, for he believed himself to be the only person who knew of these things.

"God works in mysterious ways," he told her. "I do not understand why this is happening, but I advise you to try to stop the dreaming." In time Maria de Jesus told the priest that the dreams had stopped, but only after she had experienced some dreadful nightmares. The saintly Maria lived for 30 more years and there is no further mention of her ever having any more dreams about the Southwest.

Some years later Spanish scholars came across these journal entries and were very skeptical about the stories. Surely there must be some sensible explanation. They decided to go to the convent and search the records. Convents were required to keep careful records of everyone who visited or left the convent. Perhaps Maria de Jesus, coming from a rich family, acquired the funds to visit the Southwest, and did so, merely pretending to Father Alonzo that her experiences in the New World were dreams. A careful search of the records showed that the good nun had never left the convent for the extended time that would have been necessary to make the trip and return.

The scholars then reasoned that perhaps she had sent another nun to the Southwest and used this unknown nun's experiences in describing her dreams. Again a careful and extended search was undertaken of all the convent's records to see if anyone had been absent from the convent at Agreda for the necessary length of time for such a journey. Once again the records revealed nothing.

That is the mystery. That is all the records tell us about the sightings of a beautiful, young, white woman in a nun's habit during the 1600s.

There is a third explanation that is offered today by some contemporary people. Perhaps these journal entries are an early recording of an out-of-body experience? But if it is, how is it that the Indians were able to see her and speak to her?

San Xavier del Bac, Tucson
(Courtesy Arizona Office of Tourism, Phoenix)

Each person who reads this story must decide the answer that they wish to believe. But the next time the reader has a chance to visit those marvelous ruins at Casa Grande or the lovely mission, Tumacacori, or walk through the quiet halls of the beautiful church, the white dove of the desert, San Xavier del Bac, find a quiet place and allow the atmosphere to flow over you, and then remember this story. Over three hundred years ago, a beautiful, young white woman, dressed in a flowing gown of blue, was seen visiting each of these places.

BIBLIOGRAPHY

Ayer, Mrs. Edward E., *The Memorial of Fray Alonso de Benavides, 1630*, Annotated by Frederick Webb Hodge and Charles Fletcher Lummis, Horn and Wallace, Publishers, Albuquerque, New Mexico, 1965.
Bolton, Herbert Eugene, *Rim of Christendom, A Biography, Eusebio Francisco Kino, Pacific Coast Pioneer*, The University of Arizona Press, Tucson, Arizona, 1936 and 1963.
Evans, Edna Hoffman, "The Mysterious Lady in Blue," *Arizona Highways*, September 1959.

The Sheriff Was a Major

Many of Arizona's first pioneers were people who led such interesting lives that we are captivated with their stories to this day. One such man was Major A. J. "Jim" Doran. Successful in business and the military, sheriff on the rugged frontier, a politician and leader of men, capable and tough James Doran brought to Arizona the kind of talent that helped the territory develop and flourish.

The settlers who did arrive in Arizona were often looking for new land to farm or to use for cattle ranching. There were also miners who came looking for a bonanza mineral treasure. Happenstance brought a third group to Arizona. These were the soldiers who manned the forts, protected the arriving settlers from Indian attack, forged the routes across the land, and then defended the Union during the Civil War against a Rebel force supported by friendly inhabitants from the southern part of the territory.

After their tour of duty was over, many of the soldiers elected to stay, fascinated by the possibilities of this newly-opened territory. Others went elsewhere, only to return at a later date, unable to completely shake the dust of Arizona's deserts from their hearts and minds.

Major A. J. Doran first arrived in Arizona in 1862 with a battalion of Union troops called the California Column, under the command of Colonel (later General) James H. Carleton. Carleton's orders were to rid the southern part of the territory of any Rebel troops that were stationed there. The task was accomplished after two major skirmishes, one at Stanwix Station and the other at Picacho Peak.

After the war, Major Doran returned to civilian life and spent the next 14 years engaged in mining and railroad building in California and Utah. He was involved in the completion of the first major transcontinental railroad and participated in the ceremony that finally united the two separately-built segments of track at Promontory, Utah. In San Francisco he built the first railroad turntable ever used in the United States.

The call of a newly discovered silver mine in Arizona brought him back to the territory in 1876. Arizona was to remain Major Doran's home for the rest of his long and very eventful life.

Jim Doran was hired to build the processing mill for one of the most successful silver mines in Arizona, the famous Silver King located west of Superior and north of Florence. How this huge reserve of ore was discovered is one of the grand mining stories of Arizona.

Due to Apache hostility, Camp Pinal was created near Superior for the purpose of protecting the local population. One of the soldiers, a Trooper Sullivan, had been helping to cut a trail through a nearby area. After he had completed his work for the day he started back to the camp. The day was hot, the work strenuous. A weary Sullivan sat down on a small hill to rest. While sitting there, he began to play idly with some pieces of rock by his feet. The rock consisted of heavy black fragments that would flatten when he pounded them but would not shatter. The strange quality of the rock, on further examination, intrigued him. He took a few pieces with him and returned to camp. Uncertain of what he had found, he chose not to mention his find to any of the other soldiers.

Soon afterwards, Sullivan completed his tour of duty, and having been discharged, went to the nearby town of Florence. Curious about the rock, the young soldier took a few samples to a friend of his in Florence, Charles G. Mason, to have him check them for their potential value. Mason identified the rock as rich in silver, being almost solid chloride of silver. He suggested that Sullivan go back and find a few more specimens and stake a claim to the area.

For some reason Sullivan did not do this. Some speculate that he could not find the original hill, others believe that he was killed in an Apache raid. When no legal claim surfaced, Charles Mason organized a search party of four men and himself to try to find the silver ore. For the next several years the men made periodic searches into the surrounding countryside looking for the silver outcropping. Each exploratory trip ended unsuccessfully and they were still looking for the illusive hill of silver ore in 1875. At that time it was decided that any hope of finding it was mere wishful thinking.

As the men were packing to leave from this final expedition, Mason noticed that one of the animals, a white mule, had disappeared. One of the men started to search for the lost mule and found him standing on a reddish-looking hill, sunning himself in the morning sun. When the men went up the hill to retrieve the mule, they found themselves standing on the rich black outcroppings of silver nuggets that were to become the famous Silver King Mine.

Over seven million dollars in silver were taken from the mine before the United States government repealed the Sherman Silver Purchasing Act and stopped buying silver. After this, the mine continued to operate at a lower rate of profitability. Then a most unusual incident happened.

In 1907 an old man came into the mining camp looking for work and claiming that he was Trooper Sullivan. He never explained why he had not staked a claim to the silver those many years ago. He did say that at the time he had needed to get to California and while living there he had been unable to save sufficient funds to return. When he did hear of the discovery and success of the mine, he knew that he had lost his chance to become rich. But he decided that one day he would return just to see how everything looked. The owners of the Silver King, through some old acquaintances, were able to confirm the identity of Sullivan. Financial arrangements were then made to put him on the company's payroll and provide care for him during the last few years of his life.

Charles Mason, one of the original owners, became the first superintendent of the Silver King. Major A. J. Doran, with his proven ability to lead men, which he had acquired from his military and his various railroad building experiences, was asked to become the second superintendent. At that time, many of the miners were stealing ore from the mine and the owners were concerned over the loss of income and the general lack of discipline at the Silver King. During his tenure as superintendent, Major Doran showed great determination and courage in ridding the mine of this undesirable type of miner and returned the operation to peak efficiency.

While the major was superintendent of the Silver King, Pinal County was experiencing some difficult and unsettling times. Gamblers and whiskey men, the lawless element of the county, had taken control of most of the business activities in the communities of the county. Up until 1885, Arizona was a wild, lawless country filled with robberies and murders. The current sheriff seemed unable to affect any sort of reform. The job of

Major Doran
(Courtesy Sharlot Hall Museum Archives, Prescott)

sheriff required nerves of steel, quick intelligence and a firm belief in making the fledgling legal system work. It was not an easy job.

The decent citizens living in the area were increasingly concerned for their self-protection and asked the major to run for sheriff. They had been impressed with his cool, intelligent handling of the difficulties at the Silver King. When Doran became sheriff, he demonstrated that, in spite of extreme and dangerous challenges, he was the right man to protect Pinal County.

In the years 1882 and 1883, stagecoach robberies were rampant throughout the territory. One of the most outstanding incidents concerned a stage traveling from Bisbee through Tombstone to Tucson. Fourteen thousand dollars had been taken and a man had been killed. The only evidence found at the scene of the crime was some scattered pages from a book. The sheriff of Cochise County hunted for months without success, trying to find that book and some lead about the perpetrators of the robbery and murder.

Then on August 10, 1883, the stage between Florence and Globe was robbed of $1,000 in gold and $2,000 in silver. Again a man was killed. Sheriff Doran rounded up a posse to search out clues about who had committed the robbery. At first nothing surfaced. Then someone recalled that two men (there had been two robbers) had been seen on the road to a ranch owned by a wealthy rancher named Redfield. The ranch was 75 miles from the scene of the crime. It was a gamble to travel that far to question the two men and perhaps offend the wealthy Redfield with only the barest possibility that there would be any connecting link to the robbery. Sheriff Doran decided to take the gamble. On the way to the ranch, he questioned several other people who also remembered seeing two men riding on the road just prior to the robbery and then returning shortly afterwards.

Astonishment greeted Doran and the posse when they arrived at the Redfield ranch. Not expecting anyone to come on such a tenuous lead, Redfield and one of the robbers had made no attempt to hide any evidence. Doran and the posse were easily able to find the shotgun which had been used to kill the messenger traveling on the stage. In addition, a mail sack known to have been on the stage was found. Sheriff Doran arrested the one robber who was still at the ranch as well as the rancher, Redfield. The robber quickly implicated the ranch owner as the mastermind behind the robbery and showed the posse where the silver had been hidden.

As the posse was getting the two men ready to transport to Florence, the robber told Doran that Redfield had planned other robberies and also provided protection to various criminals in return for a part of the spoils. This made the sheriff suspicious and he decided to continue searching the ranch for the possibility of finding evidence concerning other unsolved crimes. His hunch proved correct and in a small adobe outbuilding, Doran found a post in the center of the building put there ostensibly to hold up the *vegas* in the roof. It occurred to Doran that such a post was not necessary. Out of curiosity he took the post out of the ground. There, cunningly hidden in the dirt floor, he found the $14,000, as well as the missing book from the robbery which had occurred almost a year before in Cochise County.

The citizens of Florence were outraged when they found out who had been behind the rash of robberies and murders. A vigilante committee was formed which included some of the leading citizens in the town. The committee went to Sheriff Doran and demanded that he turn over the prisoners to them for hanging. Doran refused, saying that he had sufficient evidence to convict the men and that until such time as the legal process could be undertaken it was his responsibility to see to the safety of the prisoners. This he would do and anyone who attempted to take the prisoners would have to do so over his dead body.

Although the townsfolk were pleased with Doran's accomplishment, his attitude about saving the prisoners did not satisfy the members of the committee. They felt that Redfield, being a rich man, would be able to buy his way out of a conviction. It was also generally agreed that through the services of expensive lawyers, Redfield would be able to have the trial scheduled elsewhere where a jury, uninformed of the anguish that this rash of crime had caused the community, might be persuaded to allow him to escape any serious form of punishment. Doran listened sympathetically, then gave everyone his personal assurance that he would not allow the prisoners to be taken out of his protection and that a trial would indeed take place in Florence.

About ten days later, a United States marshal arrived in town with what appeared to be a posse of nine well-known gunmen. Marshal Evans had an order from the chief justice of the territory to hand over only the prisoner, Redfield, to be transported to Phoenix. The citizens in Florence felt certain that this was the beginning of a strategy to affect the release of Redfield. They wanted both prisoners kept in Florence for the trial. Sheriff Doran had a decision to make. Should he hand over the rancher, thereby breaking his word to the populace of Florence or should he refuse to honor the warrant from the chief justice?

Doran refused to obey the court order. The United States marshal threatened to take the prisoners by force. Doran summoned the citizens of the town to help him guard the jail and assist in holding the prisoners. The leading citizens of the town entered the jail at Doran's request and there the sheriff was astounded to find both prisoners hanging from the rafters of their cells, quite dead, their bodies still warm.

As an officer of the law, Doran was in a very difficult situation. He had refused to honor the warrant presented to him by a United States marshal and somehow he had not maintained careful enough security over the prisoners, and some unknown person or persons, doubtful of his ability to retain the prisoners, had taken the law into their own hands. He was twice an accessory in thwarting the law.

Major A. J. Doran had to think quickly. There was no time for the slightest hesitancy. He immediately went to the United States marshal and told him that he had reconsidered his former refusal and was now willing to release Redfield into his custody. He then conducted Marshal Evans into the jail, and opened the door to the two cells to reveal the men still hanging there lifeless. When Marshal Evans saw what had happened, he angrily said he would not take a dead Redfield back to Chief Justice Pinney.

Doran turned to the marshal. "Go back to the chief justice. Tell him that I originally refused to honor the warrant. Tell him everything that occurred, but would you write on the court order that I did offer to deliver the body?" Marshall Evans finally agreed to write the proffered offer on the warrant. As an officer of the court, Doran knew that his action was an attempt to utilize a fine point in the upholding of the law. He did not think that he would be successful, but he could come up with no alternative plan.

For awhile Florence and the county settled into a peaceful lull. Then the citation arrived. Judge Pinney ordered Sheriff Doran to appear in Phoenix to show cause why he should not be punished for contempt of court. Major Doran prepared well for his interview. When he appeared before the chief justice, he showed the written confession of the robber as well as all the evidence he had carefully amassed concerning the robberies and Redfield's involvements in the crimes. The judge studied the documents before him for a long time. Then he turned to the Major "Mr. Sheriff, go home and attend to your duties," he said. "When I want you for contempt of court I will send for you."[1]

This experience caused Major Doran to rethink his commitment to the post of sheriff and he decided not to run for the office again. But his experiences with robbers and stagecoaches

Maj. A. J. Doran
(Courtesy Arizona Historical Society Library, Tucson)

were far from over. Over the years Major Doran did a lot of traveling in the territory. The need to travel was done mostly in his capacity as a territorial official. He was elected to the territorial legislature five times and served in many leadership positions in Arizona. On October 5, 1895, Major Doran found himself the only passenger on the stage going from Florence to Casa Grande.

Suddenly, in the middle of the trip, one lone highwayman wearing a bandana over the bottom half of his face galloped up to the moving stagecoach and pointed a pistol at the driver's head.

"Stop this coach or die," he said in a harsh voice. The coachman reined in the horses to a halt.

Then the robber rode to the side of the stage, yanked open the door and pointed his pistol at Doran. "Throw up your hands and get out."

Major Doran did as he was told. The robber got off his horse and began to wave his gun erratically. While cussing furiously, he told Doran to hand over his money. Now the major was a man who did not get rattled easily. He had a $10 gold piece in his pocket and four half-dollars, which was a lot of money in those days. As cool as a cucumber, he reached into his pocket with a certain calm deliberation and brought out only the four half-dollars.

"You've got more money than that," said the robber as he grabbed the silver. "Give me the rest of your money or you die."

Doran looked at him cooly, noticing the agitated movements, the heavy-muscled body, the thick shock of black hair. "I gave you everything I have. There's nothing more to get."

The robber hesitated, giving Doran a piercing look, then he gruffly ordered the major to get back into the coach. While Doran was doing this, the robber noticed Doran's valise on the floor of the stage. "Hand over the valise," he said.

"No," answered Doran. "My valise has no money, only papers which I need."

"Don't argue with me," said the bandit, still pacing back and forth, restlessly handling the large revolver with jerking movements. "Open it."

Again Doran refused. The robber swore at the major but soon turned to the stagecoach driver. "Hand me your money."

The driver did as he was told. "Now," said the robber, "throw down the mail sack." Again the driver did as he was told.

Turning to Doran, the robber said, "Come out here and open this sack. Come quick or I'll blow your head off."

The Major stepped quickly and quietly away from the stage. "I can't open it," he said, "I don't have the key. These United States mail sacks are always locked with keys."

"So cut it open," growled the robber.

"I have a knife," said Doran turning cooly toward the bandit, "but it's against the law to open the United States mail with a knife and I don't intend to end up in jail." His attitude of indifference angered the bandit who pointed his gun at Doran, announcing that he would blow his brains out if he did not do as he was told.

Doran immediately changed his tune and started to rip open the sack, dumping the letters and small packages on the ground.

"Hell," said the robber, "I don't see any money here."

"Oh, there's money there all right," replied the Major and then as the bandit stepped closer to look, Doran made a grab for his gun, yelling to the driver to help. What happened next was a fierce life-and-death conflict between Doran and the robber as each fought for the gun. At one point, the gun went off, frightening the horses so that the driver had to struggle to keep them from running away. After about 20 minutes, the robber, who was much stronger than Doran, threw him to the ground.

Moving away from the fallen Doran, the robber turned and said, "Now I am going to kill you."

Lying in the dirt, Doran had no chance to protect himself, yet he cooly turned to the bandit and said, "It's up to you, you can kill me if you want to." For a few seconds, the steely eyes of Doran held the angry ones of the bandit and then something unexpected happened. The robber turned, and swearing mightily, mounted his horse and left.

When the robber did not return, Doran and the driver piled the mail back into the torn bag and proceeded to Casa Grande. There they informed the authorities of what had happened. A posse was formed and the robber, a man named Francisco Reina, was captured the next day and brought to trial in Florence.

The bandit turned out to be a member of a wealthy and highly respected family living in Sonora, Mexico. He had argued with his family, left home, and traveling to Arizona he had come on hard times. At the time of the robbery, Reina was without food or money.

At his trial, the jury found Reina guilty of the stagecoach robbery and another one which had occurred during the previous year. The judge and jury, tired of the constant robberies that plagued Arizona, sentenced Reina to life imprisonment on Alcatraz Island in San Francisco Harbor.

Before the prisoner was to be taken to California, he asked to meet with Major Doran. He wanted to meet with the man who was so brave as to court death in the face of a gun. During their conversation Reina told Doran that, while he was strongly tempted to kill him, he did not want to become a murderer in addition to his crimes of robbery.

Some 10 years later, Doran still remembered Reina and inquired of the warden about the prisoner. He was informed that he had been transferred to a less high security prison at San Quentin and that he was a model prisoner. Doran felt that Reina did not deserve a life sentence. But what could he do? At that time the major was in Washington, D.C. on governmental business and had an opportunity to tell President Teddy

Arizona Pioneers' Home, Prescott
(Courtesy Sharlot Hall Museum Archives)

Roosevelt the story of the robbery and ask him what action he might be able to take in the case to alleviate the harshness of the sentence. President Roosevelt sent applications of pardon to the judge who had tried Reina as well as to the United States attorney who had prosecuted him. The applications were a request for a recommendation in the situation and stated that the President would act only upon their agreement. Eventually, Reina's sentence was commuted to 12 years in prison.

After his release, Doran met Francisco Reina and the two men had dinner together in Los Angeles, where they talked over their fight in the desert. Reina returned to Mexico and eventually became a lieutenant-colonel in the federal army of Mexico.

Major Doran lived for many years in Pinal County. He built the old and the new courthouses there as well as the school. In his later years, he helped create, by legislative decree, a pioneer's home to be located in Prescott. He eventually was commissioned to build the home, and became its first superintendent. Doran resided there up to the time of his death.

From the moment Major Jim Doran entered Arizona as a military man, his adopted land tested his mettle to the fullest. His life was as rich as any metal ore found in Arizona.

[1]Doran, Colonel A. J., "Interesting Reminiscences," *Arizona Historical Review, A quarterly*, Vol. I, No. 3, Published by the Arizona State Historian, Phoenix, Arizona, October 1928, page 59.

BIBLIOGRAPHY

Abramowitz, Jack, *American History, Fifth Edition*, Follett Publishing Company, Chicago, 1970.

Arizona Weekly Enterprise, Florence, Several articles describing the robbery of the Florence-Globe stage; The visit of Marshal Evans and the Redfields hanging; Friday, August 10, 1883; August 18, 1883; Saturday, September 8, 1883.

Doran, A. J., "Interesting Reminiscences," *Arizona Historical Review, A Quarterly*, Volume I, Number 3, Published by the Arizona State Historian, Phoenix, Arizona, October 1928, pages 54-61.

Miller, Joseph, Editor, "Major Doran Gets A Pardon," based on newspaper articles from the *Prescott Journal Miner*, 1907, and the *Graham County Bulletin*, 1895, *Arizona Cavalcade, the Turbulent Times*, Hastings House Publishers, New York, 1962.

Wagoner, Jay J., *Arizona's Heritage*, Peregrine Smith, Inc., Santa Barbara and Salt Lake City, 1977.

Williams, Governor Jack, "Return of a Lost Soldier," *From the Ground Up, Stories of Arizona's Mines and Early Mineral Discoveries*, Phelps-Dodge Corporation, Douglas, Arizona, 1981.

Hattie, the
Ice-Maker's Daughter

She was a woman who believed in upholding principles in an age when women were supposed to be yielding, compromising and quiet. In Arizona it was occasionally acceptable for a bright woman during the late 1800s and early 1900s to be educated and capable. But it was always necessary to present a public picture of submission and quietude. A woman of vision who broke those unspoken rules with radical and far-reaching concepts was nearly always rejected and isolated regardless of social standing or wealth.

Hattie Lount Mosher was born in 1865. Her father, Samuel Lount, was a pioneer from Canada who came up with an original idea. Inventors are always the observers of life. They are the people who see a phenomenon that the rest of us may register, but their curiosity encourages them to explore further, often with revolutionary results. Samuel Lount was such a man.

Before 1851, if you wanted ice to chill your summer drink, you had to go to an iceman who cut blocks of ice from frozen ponds in the winter and stored the ice in sawdust until the heat of summer. Samuel, who had a curious turn of mind, noticed that ammonia gas mixed with salt water brine produced ice. Would this not be a more consistent and easier method in the long run for producing ice? With inventive skill, Samuel created our country's first ice-making machine.

Certain that his invention was a winner, Samuel was surprised when people did not come clamoring to his door to buy his machine. The businessmen and merchants, the house-wives and hotel keepers looked at him askance. "Why," they all said, "should we buy your new-fangled invention when the good Lord gives us free supplies of ice every winter?" Try as he might, Samuel got nowhere in attempting to persuade the icemen that his was a plan of the future.

Samuel Lount had a problem. Was there anywhere in the country where people would be interested in buying his machine? Was there anywhere in the United States where there was no ice in the winter which could be stored for summer use? If such a place existed, the people there would want his ice-machine. Was the newly-opened Southwest the solution to his questions and his problem?

In the early 1870s, packing up his machine and supplies, his wife, little Hattie and her brother, the Lounts moved from Michigan to Phoenix, Arizona. With a year-round summer climate, he felt certain that people would be delighted to buy his ice. Samuel built a small plant and began personally to take his ice around in a wheelbarrow trying to sell it himself. Everyone in Phoenix liked the idea of being able to get ice, but the cost of five cents a pound made it quite an expensive item for the time. Not too many people were willing to buy. Persevering in selling his product, it soon became fashionable and desirable to have ice in lemonade, ice to help preserve meat and milk, and ice to make that tasty treat, ice cream.

Samuel Lount started making money. He then expanded his business and began making and selling ice-producing machines all over the Southwest, from Globe to Tucson, from Mexico to San Francisco. In time, Samuel became a well-to-do man. With the money coming in from his ice-making business, he started buying real estate in the center of Phoenix at a time when a city block on Central Avenue was going for $400 a block. Samuel became one of the richest men in all of Arizona. By this time, in 1881, Hattie was 16 years old and her brother, William, was 18.

Pretty Hattie was given all the advantages that were available to a young girl in those early days in the emerging town of Phoenix in the Arizona territory. She was one of the first young women in the entire city to possess the luxury of a bicycle. Her wealthy and indulgent father gave her the freedom to explore everything and to learn anything that interested her. Hattie took music lessons. She learned to paint. She designed and painted the Lount logo on her father's new ice wagons. Hattie not only indulged in genteel activities that were deemed appropriate for a young woman, she also helped her father in his business. She meticulously kept the books for her father's company. She even participated in his business dealings.

It was then that her contemporaries noticed her principled ways. In business circles, it was somewhat accepted. Hattie was honest and thorough. In social circles, she was looked upon as being too stubborn for a woman, too insistent on her own opinions. This behavior was frowned upon and criticized by some. After all, women were supposed to be yielding. The art of

Hattie Lount Mosher
(Courtesy Arizona Historical Society, Central Division, Phoenix)

compromise was a nice woman's way; gentle manipulation was acceptable and even expected, but never standing stubbornly by one's convictions.

Samuel loved his feisty, capable daughter. He was proud of her accomplishments, her ability to carry on a thoughtful, intelligent, challenging conversation. He would allow no one to attempt to rein in her streak of independence. Hadn't he gone against the accepted opinions and practices of the times and hadn't he won? His daughter would do the same; as long as he was alive she could try anything, do anything, and think anything she wanted.

In 1884, when Hattie was 19, she met the handsome man-about-town, Charles Mosher, a journalist and editor of a local newspaper. Highly verbal, Charlie found himself amused and challenged by the sparkling vivacity of Hattie Lount. Their courtship glittered with excitement. Their wedding turned out to be Arizona's major social event of the year.

Everything was given to the newlyweds to insure their happiness. Hattie's parents built the couple a lovely home. The Moshers were the couple to know and invite in the social circles of Phoenix. In time, a darling daughter was born. She was called Julia after Hattie's grandmother. But the glowing romance of the marriage soon lost its luster. Some felt that Charles Mosher could not handle commitments. Others, less kind, said Hattie proved to be more than he had bargained for. One day he simply disappeared.

Disappointed, but still assured in her own sense of self, Hattie was not only able to get a divorce on the grounds of desertion, but she was also able to have the marriage annulled. Desertion was one of the few acceptable legal actions for divorce available to people at the time.

Hattie devoted herself to the raising of her daughter. When Julia grew old enough to travel, Hattie moved to Colorado where she became involved in the women's movement and also worked on the staff of the *Denver Post* newspaper. She continued in these activities for the next few years until her father died. Samuel Lount left his son, William, the ice business. He left Hattie all the real estate interests that he had acquired. Hattie Lount Mosher was now a very wealthy young woman. She had wealth enough to fulfill any dream, any fantasy. She decided to take Julia and make the grand tour of Europe.

Europe suited Hattie and her daughter. There was so much to see and do. Hattie still continued to do freelance journalism work. At one point she interviewed German Kaiser Wilhelm in Berlin. Mother and daughter pursued the study of music, a continuing and abiding love of Hattie's. They decided to settle in Germany.

Living in Europe fascinated them. Hattie was particularly taken with the range and creativity of the architecture. She was delighted with the incredible beauty of the cathedrals, palaces and public buildings. Hers was not the mere enjoyment of a tourist. She asked questions. She studied techniques. She even went so far as to learn the sewer system of Paris, which was considered by many to be the most up-to-date and innovative in the world.

But, even in Europe her sense of principle was never far from the surface. One time her mother sent her a money order for Christmas. The German postal service indicated that there would be a delivery charge of ten cents. Hattie refused to pay. "If I pay that," she said, "I won't be getting all the money my mother sent me." The postal authorities refused to relinquish the money order without the required charge. "Send it back then to Phoenix," she replied with a shrug. The German postal bureaucracy were dumbfounded. They appealed to the Phoenix postmaster, then to her mother, who laughingly refused to supply the dime. In spite of many pleas to the contrary, Hattie remained adamant. "I refuse," she repeated again and again. "It's a matter of principle to me."

When World War I broke out in Europe, Hattie and Julia returned home and Hattie began to use her restless energy to improve her many property holdings. Looking around at her home city with the knowledge of the capitals of Europe behind her, Hattie recognized that Phoenix had the potential of becoming a mecca in the Southwest. Realizing that Phoenix was in need of a new city government complex, she offered the city and the county one of the blocks she owned on Central Avenue, valued at the time at $100,000.

This was not a totally generous move on her part; she shrewdly knew that if the city accepted her offer, it would appreciably enhance the value of her surrounding properties. The city and county government did not have her vision of growth and refused her offer.

Not easily discouraged, Hattie decided to improve her various properties by adding buildings which she hoped she could rent or sell. She felt certain that Central Avenue was destined to become the apex of Phoenix and the valley. Hattie could not resist the opportunity to utilize some of the architectural designs she had admired in Europe. Why not bring these innovations to Phoenix and give the city an international flair? She built some buildings that were round in design, some were built on stilt-like structures to allow for shaded people-passages underneath, others had trees growing through the midst of the building. She even conceived the idea of building an international-class hotel that would be twice the height of any Phoenix office building of the time.

But Hattie had not reckoned with the conservative tastes of the folks living in Phoenix. Most had never seen or heard of such architectural innovations. They appeared strange and foreign in the eyes of many. Her daring was viewed as an embarrassment to people who feared being laughed at or criticized. The city, so anxious to attain acceptance among its peers, sought to copy the standard well-accepted styles of the day. Innovation might only bring derision.

Her ideas were laughed at. People gossiped about her contemptuously. "Look at that fool woman. She should be staying at home, not getting herself involved in men's business." Money to complete her half-finished buildings became scarce. Bankers who had once promised her loans based on the value of her property reneged and no longer welcomed her into their inner offices. Then things went from bad to worse.

After the war, Phoenix, with a certain lack of governmental foresight, discovered that it had fallen far behind in paving downtown streets. Business activity in the downtown sections of the town was being negatively affected. To catch up fast was the political charge of the moment. Property owners all over downtown Phoenix were heavily assessed to help pay for the new pavements. For someone with so much property in the center of town, Hattie's assessments, in addition to her spiraling building expenses, proved too much to handle. In addition, her

Hattie Mosher and the first bicycle in Phoenix.
(Courtesy of the Arizona Historical Society, Central Division, Phoenix)

brother had recently died, leaving her the ice business which she felt was being taxed unfairly and not in keeping with its true worth. Everywhere she turned, problems confronted her.

She decided to seek legal redress for her problems. She went to court to protest. She was determined to prevail. Surely as a business owner and a property owner, she had some rights, some avenue of relief from arbitrary political dictates.

Whether Hattie was given bad advice by her attorney or whether she chose to ignore the advice we don't know. We do know that she took to studying the law, and she continued to bring to court case after case in hopes of winning her cause. She even attempted to achieve a political office in order to influence the governmental mind-set of the day. She ran unsuccessfully for city commissioner in 1920 and for the state Senate in 1922.

Soon her fortune began to be eaten away by burgeoning legal fees. Liens were placed on her properties. Foreclosures began to occur for non-payment of taxes. For Hattie, who had always had ample money all of her life, this was a bewildering time. Still she continued to fight for her rights and her cause. "Fighting doesn't pay," she once wrote to her mother, "but it is the only way that I can get positive and authentic information. Otherwise all one hears is bureaucratic babbling." At one point, Hattie was thrown in jail for not giving in. This resulted in headlines in newspapers throughout the state, "Arizona's Wealthiest Woman Behind Bars."

This proud, aging woman found herself slipping slowly into poverty. When her daughter Julia died in childbirth, Hattie became even more of a loner and a recluse, living frugally in the basement of one of her remaining buildings. Over the decades, people grew used to seeing her eccentric figure dressed in faded Victorian finery walking the streets of downtown Phoenix with her bag for collecting scraps of food.

But even that small bit of security was finally to be taken from her. She was evicted from her basement home when the building was sold to satisfy unpaid taxes. Bewildered, Hattie wondered if she would have to live on the streets. The new owner of her property found her a small room nearby. Somehow she continued to manage, determined still in her loneliness.

When she was 80 years old, some burglars broke into her apartment, convinced that this little old eccentric but formerly wealthy lady must be hiding money. They severely beat her, trying to make her tell the whereabouts of a hidden hoard of wealth. All they found was a basket of overripe strawberries.

Between the beating and a fall later that year, Hattie became too weak to care for herself. She was too fragile to undergo an operation. Blood transfusions and other efforts came too late. She died in November, 1945.

Perhaps Hattie Lount Mosher was a woman before her time, perhaps she was too blindly stubborn to the realities surrounding her; no one knows for certain. But, she dared to break the unspoken rules of her time: women were to be seen, to be charming, to be submissive. She dared to be eccentric and say, "But, it's a matter of principle."

BIBLIOGRAPHY

Finnerty, Margaret, "Stubborn Hattie," *Scottsdale Progress Saturday Magazine*, November 29, 1986, pages 3-5.

Johnson, G. Wesley Jr., *Phoenix, Valley of the Sun*, Continental Heritage Press, Inc., Tulsa, Oklahoma, 1982.

Letters from Hattie Mosher to her mother, Mrs. Julia Lount, August 21, 1905 to November 6, 1905. Arizona Historical Foundation. Small Collection, Box 1/1, Gift of Mr. Stewart, Carl Hayden Library, Arizona State University, Tempe, Arizona.

The Great Desert Automobile Race

In 1989, Phoenix became the host city of a Grand Prix international automobile race. For weeks prior to the event, the media ballyhooed the upcoming contest. The fastest cars and the finest drivers were coming to town to compete for millions in prize money. Phoenix was finally going big time. No one seemed to recollect that Phoenix had once before, in the dawn of automobile history, hosted a great automobile race.

It was during the years from 1908 to 1914 that Phoenix joined with Los Angeles to sponsor a series of Great Desert Races. These automobile races were the brainchild of two men, John Purdy Bullard, the attorney general of the Territory of Arizona, and John W. Mitchell, general manager of a well-known Los Angeles hotel, the Hollenbeck. The purpose of these races was not only to bring attention to the two cities, but to graphically illustrate the need to fund the building of a road between them.

Bullard and Mitchell, recognizing the need to generate publicity for a contest using such a comparatively new invention as the automobile, persuaded Dr. George Vickers, owner of the *Arizona Republican* newspaper, to co-sponsor the race. The course was to be approximately 500 miles long over some of the roughest desert and mountain terrain to be found anywhere. In places, the road was no more than a wagon track. Few accouterments of civilization were to be found anywhere along the route. There would be no back-up teams to supply every automotive need. There would be few places for spectators to watch. The only prizes would be two silver cups.

During this time, a young man named Ralph Hamlin was trying to earn a living selling automobiles in Los Angeles. He had recently been able to persuade the manufacturers of the Franklin air-cooled car to give him the distributorship for Southern California. Hamlin hoped to sell many cars by convincing his customers about the advantages of an air-cooled car in the Southwest's climate. All of his competitors were selling water-cooled cars. Despite its promise, the Franklin was a new, untested car and often his competitors would win a sale away from Hamlin by asking the prospective customer, "If air-cooled automobiles are so great, why is everyone else selling only water-cooled cars?"

Hamlin had to come up with a strategy to overcome this selling liability. His plan was to enter every car race he could find and pit the Franklin against the pack to win. During a regular meeting of car distributors in California, Hamlin first heard of the impending Los Angeles-Phoenix Desert Race. Immediately interested in getting in on the action, Hamlin inquired how he could participate. His query brought hoots of derision from several men who had been discussing the contest. Then Captain Ryus, a White Steamer distributor, speaking to the assembled group with a contemptuous tone, stated that an air-cooled Franklin could not possibly get across a desert.

Ryus's challenging words only hardened Hamlin's determination. When Hamlin attempted to sell the Franklin, constant badgering by the other distributors only fueled his resolve. There were already three cars entered in the race: a White Steamer, a Kissel Kar and an Elmore. Each automobile was to be driven by one of the finest sportsmen of the time.

An underdog, Hamlin became the fourth contestant. In comparison to such driving greats of the day as Colonel Fenner and Bert Latham, Hamlin was totally unknown and rarely mentioned in the pre-racing publicity. With only determination and faith in his machine, Hamlin prepared for the big day.

The race began at midnight. A big crowd cheered as each contestant left the front of the Hollenbeck Hotel a scheduled five minutes apart. Large crowds had gathered to line the roads through town. The excitement among the spectators seemed more than usual for racing enthusiasts. Perhaps people sensed that history was being made. This race would echo into the future as the harbinger of a new form of competition.

For Hamlin, the race was to provide him with a chance to prove the Franklin's worth and to gain the respect of the other auto dealers. The trail, though well-defined, was rough and sandy, but he managed to make good time through Palm Springs and Indio. It was almost daylight when Hamlin and his mechanic, Guy Erwin, passed the northern edge of the Salton Sea to reach Banning. Having been the last to leave the starting line, Hamlin had not yet encountered any of the other cars.

The route grew rough as they entered a steep canyon. It was

then that Hamlin spotted his first competitor, the Kissel Kar, hopelessly stuck in the sand. He wondered if he should just pass on, but decided to stop his automobile. It took the power of both cars and the concerted effort of both crews to get the Kissel Kar out. "Hey, Ralph," said Harris Hanshue, the mechanic of the Kissel Kar, "don't you know that there's a race going on?" Hamlin answered, "I may be in the same fix sometime, Harry; it's not so good to be stuck 200 miles from nowhere." In those few moments Hamlin made a lifetime friend and supporter.

The course was filled with mishaps as the racers dodged ruts, rocks, sand and washes. By this time, Hamlin was puzzled as to where the other drivers were getting their water to keep their engines cooled. Then he noticed a large rag tied to a bush. Hidden under the bush was a five-gallon can of water. Smaller rags warned of bad bumps or obstructions in the road.

At Blythe, Hamlin had only a short run to the river and the overnight control point where he would receive his final timed speed for the day. Here they would stay for the night and in the morning be ferried across the Colorado River. But darkness comes swiftly to the desert, and before they realized what was happening, they were hopelessly lost in the blackness of a desert night. Low on gas, they were forced to quit short of reaching the control point. They had to wait until morning to find the road to the Colorado. This meant that they had no chance of winning.

But Hamlin felt that he could not allow the Franklin's automotive ability to continue being challenged. A question still needed to be answered. Could an air-cooled car make it across the desert? Even though Hamlin knew they weren't going to be able to win, he decided to go on to Phoenix to prove that the air-cooled Franklin automobile could indeed cross the Southwestern desert.

On Monday, November 9, 1908, at 6:00 p.m., the whistle on top of the Phoenix Electric Light and Power Company building sounded a series of blasts. That was the signal to clear the traffic off Adams Street from the state capitol to the downtown area. All horse-drawn vehicles, bicycles and pedestrians were shunted to side streets. One of the racers had been sighted entering Phoenix. A crowd formed along Adams. Little boys climbed into trees for a better view. At 6:30 p.m. a voice shouted, "Here he comes!"

Colonel Fenner's White Steamer, barely discernible in a thick cloud of dust, drove into view, stopping in front of the offices of the *Arizona Republican* newspaper. The race was over. It had taken 30 hours and 20 minutes of actual running time. Approximately an hour later, the Kissel Kar came in to win second place in the race.

All four automobiles made it through the race. Hamlin's Franklin arrived last, coming in at 9:50 p.m. just about three hours after the winner. Hamlin had proved that an air-cooled car could go the distance.

A finish was formally recreated on Thursday afternoon at the territorial fairgrounds. A packed crowd in the grandstands gave the racers a rousing ovation. The governor of the territory congratulated the contestants. That evening a banquet was held at the Adams Hotel to honor the teams. Afterwards, the racers retired to the Louvre Bar next door where they began a tradition that was to be continued after all future races. The prized silver trophy was filled and refilled with champagne until everyone had drunk their fill.

Later, the automobiles were shipped back to Los Angeles and the teams returned by train. On the train back to Los Angeles, Ralph Hamlin, encouraged rather than disheartened, was already planning his strategy for the 1909 race.

The same contestants entered the 1909 race. But now the line-up included ten cars with such names as Studebaker, Ford and Buick. Again the start-up was in front of the Hollenbeck Hotel, this time at 10:00 p.m. on November 6. Ralph Hamlin chose to drive a newer version of the Franklin, the H Model. He chose as his mechanic, Clayton Carris, a man experienced in desert travel. This time the route went south of the Salton Sea toward Yuma. Hamlin felt that he had a good start. Things were looking favorable for a competitive race and his spirits were high.

At Brawley, in the excitement of making unexpectedly good speed, Hamlin drove too fast over a railroad crossing and smashed the Franklin's differential housing. There was no hope of repair. Hamlin was out of the race. Of the ten cars that started, only four finished the 400-mile course. The winning car was a Buick, driving the distance in just over 19 hours and averaging speeds of up to 25 miles per hour.

By now the Los Angeles-Phoenix Desert Races were becoming famous throughout the country and Hamlin could not walk away from the challenge. He was determined not to give up. When the 1910 race was scheduled, he was among the 14 entries. Not only did many of the prior contestants sign up, but because the race was generating so much interest, several manufacturers entered their cars for the first time. Among the starters were a Velie, a Rambler, an Ohio, a Maxwell and a Mercer. A train nicknamed the "Howdy Special" had even been chartered to allow spectators to follow the race, rendezvousing with the racers at the night control point and meeting them at the finish.

This time Hamlin was a mere 32 minutes behind the winning Kissel Kar driven by Harvey Herrick. Progressing from finishing last in one race, to a wipe-out in another, and now coming in second, Hamlin recognized that he was beginning to be considered a serious racing contender and his Franklin an automobile to be reckoned with.

By the 1911 race, betting on the automobiles by the racers and the spectators reached an all-time high. Ralph decided to bet on himself and the Franklin in order to try to cover the considerable expenses involved in participating. Once again, victory eluded him and he came in second behind Harvey Herrick driving a National.

In 1912, Ralph Hamlin decided to take stock of the situation. He had come in second place twice. He had proven that an air-cooled car would survive the worst that a southwestern desert could offer. What were his options? He could give up competing, saying that he had proven enough about the Franklin. He was after all a salesman and technically he had shown that the Franklin was a good car. Or, he could quit fooling around and win the damn race!

Hamlin began to make his plans carefully. As part of his strategy, he would really do his homework. This time he was determined that nothing would keep him from winning. Before the race, he drove the entire course, trying out several speeds at different places, estimating carefully just how fast he could go and just how much he could get away with. After this test run, he calculated the distance and the times he felt he could do on each segment of the course. He reckoned that he could win the race in a time of 18 hours and 10 minutes, barring an accident. Now all he had to do was do it.

On Saturday, October 26, an hour before midnight, the race began. Twelve drivers were ready; twelve restless mechanics nervously inspected pressure pumps and controls. Before the men were 511 miles of desert, sand, shrubs, cactus, mountains and streams of water.

But for the moment, there was excitement. People crowded around the cars asking questions, officials pompously conversed in whispers about the seemingly weighty matters of the racing game. Twenty-four beams of light pierced the night sky diminishing the sparkle of the stars above Los Angeles. At the same time 20 cars were being readied to leave San Diego to compete as well. This race was to be a double-header.

At 11:05 p.m., the first driver was given a sharp slap on his back, the signal to start. Hamlin was ninth to leave the starting line. All his energy, all his concentration, was bent on catching up with the eight skilled, experienced drivers in front of him. As he drove through Los Angeles, he reviewed his plan. The bigger, higher-powered cars would speed up over the relatively decent roads outside of Los Angeles; it was when they hit the desert trails, that Hamlin figured that his lighter Franklin would be able to outmaneuver and pass them. Hamlin's mechanic, Andrew Smith, hand-focused a huge searchlight, constantly maneuvering it to illuminate at least 200 yards in front of them.

At about 53 miles into the course, they came across the first accident. A Buick lay in the center of the road, a twisted mass of broken steel. Quick reflexes enabled Hamlin to barely avoid colliding with the overturned car. A Mercedes that had been following Hamlin was not so lucky and two cars were finished with the race.

Outside of Banning, Hamlin's mechanic shouted to him, "There are only four ahead of us now, only four." They soon passed two Cadillacs. Now only a Simplex and another Cadillac were ahead of them.

Then a sandstorm came out of nowhere, the sand slashing at their faces. The wind and cold left them exhausted as grueling mile after grueling mile flashed by. Then they heard the bad news: storms had swollen rivers and streams to raging, impassable barriers. Was his chance at victory to be snatched away once more? No ferry was available, no bridge existed.

Racing car similar to those used in the Great Desert Automobile Race, November 7, 1915. Winning driver is C. A. Bennett.
(Courtesy Arizona Historical Society, Tucson, from Buehman Collection)

The next morning, Hamlin started out determined to push on in spite of the reported conditions ahead. He and his mechanic soon found themselves facing a flooding Hassayampa River. Testing the depth of the water, they found it to be about two-feet deep. Hamlin decided to chance it and plunged the Franklin into the river. He was able to plow across the raging torrent to the other side. Hamlin smiled. Nothing would stop him now.

Then he came to the Agua Fria River, where the flooding was more severe. He stopped the car, wrapped the generator with a rubber cover, hired four horses and had the Franklin towed across. After all that, Hamlin had only a 20-minute lead, with the Simplex and the Cadillac too close for comfort.

It was then that he saw in the distance the town of Phoenix rise into view like the mythical bird, its namesake. With a burst of speed, he raced into the fairgrounds and circled the track. Ralph Hamlin had won! His estimated time of 18 hours and 10 minutes was off from his real time by a mere 22 seconds. He had bested the record, averaging 28 miles an hour for 511 miles. The crowd at the fairgrounds rose to their feet and cheered. The "Howdy" crowd from the Los Angeles train raised him to their shoulders and rode him around the fairgrounds. He had won! It was a moment of triumph.

Ralph Hamlin did not compete in the last two of the six desert races that were held in 1913 and 1914. He had proven his car. He had proven himself. He continued to successfully sell the Franklin air-cooled car until the manufacturers went bankrupt during the Great Depression. Aside from being a racing driver great, Hamlin is credited with developing an innovative idea that was to revolutionize the American marketplace. He was the first person to initiate the concept of buying a car on the time payment plan.

Once again the sounds of racing cars and the cheering of crowds is being heard in Phoenix. There will always be newer forms of automobile racing competition. Will these new contests reverberate through time as well as those past moments of courage and bravery?

BIBLIOGRAPHY

James E. Cook, "Automobile Was a Horse of Another Color," *The Arizona Republic*, Sunday, January 8, 1989.

Etta Gifford Young, "A Classic Auto Race," *Arizona, The New State Magazine*, Volume II, October 1912.

Ralph Hamlin, "The Great Desert Race," *Desert, Magazine of the Southwest*, Vol. 25, Number 10, October 1962, pages 22-27.

Lowell Parker, "Motorized Daredevils Braved Untracked Desert in 1908 Race," *Arizona Republican Newspaper*, December 8, 1975.

Lowell Parker, "All Four Starters in First L.A.-Phoenix Event Finished," *Arizona Republican Newspaper*, December 9, 1975.

Lowell Parker, "The Race is Over, Herrick Wins, But Where Are Seven Cars," *Arizona Republican Newspaper*, December 10, 1975.

Jay J. Wagoner, *Arizona's Heritage*, Peregrine Smith, Inc., Santa Barbara and Salt Lake City, 1977, page 251.

A Sheriff Meets the Woodson Brothers

People often complain about how difficult teenagers are nowadays.

The list of objections can include quite a range of offending behavior. They never listen, they are too wild, don't respect authority, are very self-involved, lazy and all they ever think about is money. Sometimes when this type of conversation is underway, there is added a poignant wish that teenagers today could be more like the youngsters back in the olden times, back in the days when Arizona was still a territory.

This is the story of two teenage boys, the Woodson brothers. In April of 1910, they were living in the Phoenix area. At that time Ernest Woodson was 18 years old and his brother Oscar was 16. The brothers found themselves without any money. They were not at all happy about being without funds. What teenager likes being without cash? Every minute of their time was devoted to thinking up ways to get some funds. They applied for all kinds of employment. The jobs that were available at the time all required hard work. If hard labor wasn't the main condition of employment, the position usually demanded long hours. Oscar and Ernie didn't like to work hard and they surely didn't like to work long hours. What they wanted was a way to make money that would be fun, exciting, wouldn't take too much effort and would give them quick cash.

During the month of April, when balmy breezes created small dust devils, the brothers, lounging comfortably in the shade, spent hours discussing their problem and all the possible ways of solving it. Suggestion after suggestion was rejected. Finally one day Oscar exclaimed, "I know what we can do! It's just come to me."

"What," retorted Ernie, feeling hopelessly languid in the heat of an afternoon.

"We can rob a train," said Oscar enthusiastically. "There hasn't been a train robbery in the territory for as long as I can remember, no one will be expecting one. It should be so easy."

"Rob a train?" questioned Ernie, sarcasm dripping from his voice. "How are we going to rob a train? We don't have enough

Sheriff Carl Hayden (Courtesy Arizona Historical Foundation, Hayden Library, Arizona State University, Tempe)

money to buy us a ticket to get on a train."

"Now wait a minute," Oscar replied, "we don't need a lot of money to buy some tickets for the shuttle train that goes from Phoenix to Maricopa. All that takes is a few bits of change. We can manage that."

The Woodson boys spent hours planning their strategy. Ernie was soon caught up in Oscar's enthusiasm. Finally they were ready to put their plan into action.

On the morning of May 11, 1910, the brothers went into Phoenix and rented two horses and two revolvers. Then they rode their newly rented horses along the railroad tracks to a point about 15 minutes out of the Phoenix station. There they tied their mounts to some greasewood shrubs and proceeded to walk back to Phoenix.

Later that afternoon Oscar and Ernie purchased two tickets for the shuttle train leaving Phoenix at 6:10 p.m. When the train pulled out of the station heading for Maricopa, it was crowded with territorial officials coming home after a legislative session and people coming home after work. Among the passengers were the attorney general of the territory and the sheriff of Gila County. Also on board the train were the Woodson brothers.

As the train approached the place where Ernie and Oscar had left their horses, both boys pulled out their revolvers, stuck them in the belly of the conductor and told him to stop the train.

Fearing for his life, the conductor stopped the train. With cool aplomb, the brothers proceeded to rob the passengers, the territorial officials, the sheriff of Gila County, and even the train crew of their valuables and money. In all, they took about $300 worth of money, watches and jewels.

The boys then pistol-whipped one of the passengers to discourage anyone from attempting to stop them, jumped off the train and onto their horses, and rode south across the desert toward the Mexican border.

In under two hours, the sheriff of Maricopa County, Carl Hayden, had organized a posse. He had also made arrangements for a special train to start from Phoenix. Attached to the train was a cattle car. Sheriff Hayden put the posse on the train and their horses in the cattle car and they rode to the scene of the crime. There they saw, scattered along the side of the track, slashed wallets and torn purses. Disappearing into the desert were easily identifiable hoofprints.

The posse saddled up their horses and, with the aid of two Pima Indian trackers, headed across the desert in hot pursuit. The only person to get back on the train besides the crew was Sheriff Carl Hayden. He ordered the train to continue on to the town of Maricopa.

When the sheriff arrived in Maricopa, he went to visit a man named J. F. McCarthy, the proprietor of a local hotel. "J. F.," said Sheriff Hayden, "I understand that you own an automobile."

"Yup," replied J. F. McCarthy, "I own a Stoddard-Dayton automobile. Cost me $3,000. It's the fastest car in the territory."

"I want to draft your automobile into my posse," said the sheriff.

"You want to draft my automobile into your posse?" questioned the surprised owner. "Why?"

"Because it is May, and you know how hot it gets out on the desert at this time of year. If my posse doesn't catch those robbers soon, their horses are going to get hot, tired and thirsty. The horses won't be able to continue. Now if I had your automobile," continued the sheriff, "it would not get hot, tired and thirsty and we could continue the chase until we catch 'em. J. F., I need your automobile."

"Well," replied the hotel owner, frowning thoughtfully, "you can have it on one condition—I have to drive."

"Done," said Sheriff Carl Hayden rising from his chair.

The two men jumped into the Stoddard-Dayton which was parked behind the hotel and, stopping only long enough to pick up a United States customs official who knew every watering hole from Maricopa to the Mexican border, proceeded to careen up and down arroyos, speeding around cactus and racing

A 1910 Stoddard-Dayton, like the automobile used by Sheriff Carl Hayden as part of his posse that apprehended the Woodson brothers.
(Courtesy Arizona Historical Society, Tucson. Photo by Tenney Williams)

through greasewood shrubs. They soon caught up with the posse in a Papago village where they found the men's hot and thirsty horses.

Sheriff Hayden called to a couple of his deputies to jump in the car and they continued south, following the Woodson brothers' tracks. The trail through the desert was easy to follow, as the brothers, certain of their success, had made no serious attempt to cover their route. Eventually their tracks turned into a sandy arroyo, for the Woodson boys' horses were also hot and thirsty, and they needed a rest.

When the brothers saw the cloud of dust from the approaching car, they thought that the automobile belonged to some rich miners out for a joy ride. They came out of their hiding place and called for help.

The Stoddard-Dayton came to a screeching halt and the deputies jumped out of the car, raised their revolvers and aimed them at the boys, ready to fire.

"Put up your hands," yelled one of the deputies, "or I'll shoot."

Ernie put up his hands to surrender. But Oscar kept his hand firmly in his pocket, fingering his revolver.

"Throw up your hands," the deputy growled, cocking his pistol.

"Now wait a minute, Billy," said Sheriff Carl Hayden, "I don't want anyone hurt if I can help it." The sheriff then raised his revolver, which happened to be unloaded, and with a calm, steady voice called to Oscar, "Raise up your hands son. As I said, I don't want anyone hurt if I can help it."

For a long minute Oscar hesitated. Then, deciding that living was the wiser course, he slowly raised his hands.

In under 20 hours, the Woodson brothers were handcuffed and in captivity. The Stoddard-Dayton had acquired a flat and the boys were returned to Phoenix by train.

When the people of Phoenix heard of the capture of the robbers by Sheriff Hayden, with the aid of an automobile, the city went wild with excitement. People gathered around the railroad depot and later at the courthouse to see Carl Hayden bring the captives in. Everyone cheered their cool, efficient sheriff who was forward-looking enough to dare to use an automobile for the first time as a part of a posse.

In time, a federal judge found Oscar and Ernest Woodson guilty of horse stealing and armed robbery, and the brothers were sentenced to ten years in a Kansas penitentiary. They served there for 3½ years before being released on probation. What happened to the Woodson brothers after that has been lost in history, but Sheriff Carl Hayden went on a few years later to be elected to the United States Congress when Arizona first became a state. Carl Hayden continued to serve the citizens of Arizona in the United States Congress for 56 years, first as a member of the House of Representatives and then as a Senator. Carl Hayden served his country in Congress longer than any other man.

What a fascinating life that man lived! Born in the days when Arizona was a territory, he lived during the Apache raids, during the OK Corral incident and the Pleasant Valley feuds. He saw Arizona go from a territory to a state. He lived through World War I, the Great Depression, World War II, the Korean War, the Vietnam War and lived long enough to turn his television set on and watch an American man step onto the moon. Carl Hayden, a pioneer and cool-headed sheriff, is remembered as a dedicated first citizen of Arizona.

BIBLIOGRAPHY

August, Jack J. Jr., "A Sterling Young Democrat. Carl Hayden's Road to Congress, 1900-1912," *The Journal of Arizona History*, Arizona Historical Society, Volume 28, Number 5, Autumn 1987, pages 217-242.
Cook, James E., "Great Arizona Road Once Belonged to Maytag." *The Arizona Republic*, Sunday, June 25, 1989, page E-2.
Cook, James E., "Ruthless People," *The Arizona Republic*, Sunday, March 5, 1989, page F-27.
Trimble, Marshall, *In Old Arizona*, Golden West Publishers, Phoenix, Arizona, 1985.

Index

Outdoor books from Golden West

Western history from Golden West

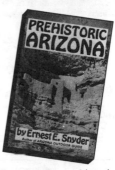

A guide to the how and why of prehistoric events, the ruins of ancient civilizations in Arizona and their artifacts. Complete with photographs, maps, charts and index.

Prehistoric Arizona
by Dr. Ernest E. Snyder (128 pages)...$5.00

The way it really was, by a Southwest historian-journalist—Esteban's life among the Zuni, Pancho Villa's raid north of the border, Mark Twain's drug scheme, the strange death of Ambrose Bierce, etc.

Southwest Saga
by William C. McGaw (160 pages)...$5.00

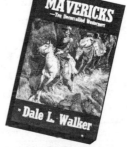

Ten uncorralled Westerners—the strays, the loners, the exceptional. "They appeal to the rebel...the barbarian...in all of us," says Sonnichsen. They include writers, soldiers of fortune and iconoclasts.

Mavericks
by Dale L. Walker (120 pages)...$5.00

Daring deeds and exploits of Wyatt Earp, Buckey O'Neill, the Rough Riders, Arizona Rangers, cowboys, Power brothers shootout, notorious Tom Horn, Pleasant Valley wars, the Hopi revolt—action-packed true tales of early Arizona!

Arizona Adventure
by Marshall Trimble (160 pages)...$5.00

Real-life thrilling adventures from the history books; pre-statehood Arizona, on the Overland Trail, at Apache Pass, Dragoon Spring, Maricopa Wells, Morgan's Ferry, Oatman Flat, Filibuster Camp. Events on The Devil's Highway, Soldier Holes, Fort Moroni, Fort Misery.

Old West Adventures in Arizona
by Charles D. Lauer (160 pages)... $5.95

ORDER BLANK

Golden West Publishers

4113 N. Longview Ave. Phoenix, AZ 85014

Please ship the following books:

Number of Copies		Per Copy	AMOUNT
	Arizona Adventure	5.00	
	Arizona—Off the Beaten Path	5.00	
	Arizona Legends and Lore	5.95	
	Arizona Outdoor Guide	5.95	
	Bill Williams Mountain Men	5.00	
	Conflict at the Border	5.00	
	Cowboy Slang	5.00	
	Destination: Grand Canyon	5.00	
	Discover Arizona	5.00	
	Explore Arizona	5.00	
	Ghost Towns in Arizona	5.00	
	Hiking Arizona	5.95	
	In Old Arizona	5.00	
	Mavericks	5.00	
	Old West Adventures in Arizona	5.95	
	On the Arizona Road	5.00	
	Prehistoric Arizona	5.00	
	Quest for the Dutchman's Gold	6.95	
	Southwest Saga	5.00	
	Verde River Recreation Guide	5.95	
	Wild West Characters	5.95	
Add $1.50 to total order for shipping & handling			$1.50

Check (or money order) enclosed...$_____

Name _____

Address _____

City _____ State _____ Zip _____

This order blank may be photo-copied.